WILLIAM WORDSWORTH

Andrew Keanie

GE
H EXCHANGE
NDON

Greenwich Exchange, London

First published in Great Britain in 2000
Reprinted 2005
All rights reserved

William Wordsworth
© Andrew Keanie 2005

Printed and bound by Q3 Digital/Litho, Loughborough
Tel: 01509 213456
Typesetting and layout by Albion Associates, London
Tel: 020 8852 4646
Cover design by December Publications, Belfast
Tel: 028 90286559

Cover: Mary Evan Picture Library

Greenwich Exchange Website: www.greenex.co.uk

ISBN 1-871551-57-9

To Eleanor, with love

CONTENTS

	Brief Chronology	6
I	Perspective	9
II	The 1790s Pre-Visionary Development	15
III	The Importance of Wordsworth's Relationship with Coleridge	37
IV	The Image of the Poet	53
V	The Aesthetics of Fear and Depression in the Lake District	60
VI	William and Dorothy	73
VII	The Significance of the 1802 Preface to *Lyrical Ballads*	78
VIII	An Unwelcome *Excursion*	82
IX	Later Works	90
X	In Conclusion	100
	Footnotes	105
	Select Bibliography	106

The 'experiment', we think, has failed, not because the language of conversation is little adapted to 'the purposes of poetic pleasure', but because it has been tried upon uninteresting subjects. Yet every piece discovers genius; and, ill as the author has frequently employed his talents, they certainly rank him with the best of living poets.

Robert Southey.
From a review of *Lyrical Ballads*, *The Critical Review*, XXIV, October 1798.

A poet in our time is a semi-barbarian in a civilized community. He lives in the days that are past. His ideas, thoughts, feelings, associations, are all with barbarous manners, obsolete customs, and exploded superstitions. The march of his intellect is like that of a crab, backward. The brighter the light diffused around him by the progress of reason, the thicker is the darkness of antiquated barbarism, in which he buries himself like a mole, to throw up the barren hillocks of his Cimmerian labours. The philosophic mental tranquillity which looks round with an equal eye on all external things, collects a store of ideas, discriminates their relative value, assigns to all their proper place, and from the materials of useful knowledge thus collected, appreciated, and arranged, forms new combinations that impress the stamp of their power and utility on the real business of life, is diametrically the reverse of that frame of mind which poetry inspires, or from which poetry can emanate. The highest inspirations of poetry are resolvable into three ingredients: the rant of unregulated passion, the wining of exaggerated feeling, and the cant of factitious sentiment: and can therefore serve only to ripen a splendid lunatic like Alexander, a puling driveller like Werter, or a morbid dreamer like Wordsworth.

Thomas Love Peacock.
From 'The Four Ages of Poetry' (1820).

No storm, no shipwreck startles us by its horrors: but the rainbow lifts its head in the cloud, and the breeze sighs through the withered fern. No sad vicissitude of fate, no overwhelming catastrophe in nature deforms his page: but the dewdrop glitters on the bending flower, the tear collects in the glistening eye.

William Hazlitt.
From 'Mr Wordsworth', *The Spirit of the Age* (1825).

I see in Wordsworth the Natural Man rising up against the Spiritual Man continually, and then he is No Poet but a Heathen Philosopher at Enmity against all true Poetry or Inspiration.

William Blake.
An 1826 annotation toWordsworth's *Poems* (vol. 1, 1815).

I brought home and read *The Prelude*. It is a poorer *Excursion*, the same sort of faults and beauties; but the faults greater, and the beauties fainter, both in themselves and because faults are always made more offensive and beauties less pleasing by repetition. The story is the old story. There are the old raptures about mountains and cataracts; the old flimsy philosophy about the effect of scenery upon the mind; the old crazy, mystical metaphysics; the endless wilderness of dull, flat, prosaic twaddle; and here and there fine descriptions and energetic declamations interspersed.

Thomas Babington MaCauley (1800-1859).
From an entry in his Journal, July 1850.

Nature had endowed him with the poet's gift of seeing more than ordinarily far into the brick walls of external reality, of intuitively comprehending the character of the bricks, of feeling the quality of their being, and establishing the appropriate relationship with them. But he preferred to think his gifts away. He preferred, in the interests of preconceived religious theory, to ignore the disquieting strangeness of things, to interpret the impersonal diversity of Nature in terms of a divine, Anglican unity. He chose, in a word, to be a philosopher, comfortably at home with a man-made and, therefore, thoroughly comprehensible system, rather than a poet adventuring for adventure's sake through the mysterious world revealed by his direct and undistorted intuitions.

Aldous Huxley (1894-1963).
From 'Wordsworth in the Tropics', 1929.

Brief Chronology

1770   Wordsworth born 7 April at Cockermouth, Cumberland.

1771   Dorothy Wordsworth, his sister, born 25 September.

1778   Mother, Ann Wordsworth, dies.

1779   Enters Hawkshead Grammar School, near Esthwaite Lake. Lodges at Ann Tyson's cottage.

1783   Father, John Wordsworth, dies.

1787-91 Enters St John's College, Cambridge.

1790   Walking tour in France and Switzerland with Robert Jones (July-October).
Edmund Burke's *Reflections on the Revolution in France* published.

1791-92 Lives in France. Supports French Revolution. Love affair with Annette Vallon. Daughter, Caroline, born in December 1792. Composes *Descriptive Sketches*.

1793   Publishes *An Evening Walk and Descriptive Sketches*.
Louis XVI executed in January.
War declared between England and France in February.
Wordsworth writes his open *Letter to the Bishop of Llandaff*, but doesn't publish it.
William Godwin's *Political Justice* published.
British Government clamps down on sedition and dissent.

1794   William and Dorothy together again at Windy Brow, Keswick.
Robespierre executed 28 July.
Wordsworth nurses Raisley Calvert.

1795   Calvert dies. Leaves Wordsworth £900.
Coleridge lecturing in Bristol.
Wordsworth visiting Godwin frequently.
Wordsworth settles at Racedown, Dorset, with Dorothy.

1797   Completes *The Borderers*.
Moves to Alfoxden, nearer Coleridge.
Annus mirabilis (1797-8).

1798 *Lyrical Ballads* published.
William, Dorothy and Coleridge go to Germany.
Wordsworth writes foundation of *The Prelude* during the
cold, lonely winter months at Goslar.

1799 Settles at Dove Cottage, Grasmere, with Dorothy.

1800 Second edition of *Lyrical Ballads* (published January 1801).
Writes Preface.

1802 Marries Mary Hutchinson.
Wordsworth able (because of Peace of Amiens) to visit Annette
and Caroline (in August).

1803 War resumes. Growing fear of invasion.
First son, John, born.

1804 Coleridge sets sail for Malta. *The Prelude* grows out of its five-
book format.
Napoleon crowns himself Emperor.

1805 Wordsworth's brother John, Captain of the *Earl of Abergavenny*,
drowned.
Wordsworth completes thirteen-book *Prelude*. Doesn't publish.

1806-7 Wordsworth reads *Prelude* to an unhealthy looking Coleridge
(on the latter's having just returned from Malta).
Poems in Two Volumes published in 1807.

1809 Publishes *The Convention of Cintra*.

1810 Son, William, born.
Estranged from Coleridge.

1813 Takes job as tax collector for Westmorland. Moves to Rydal
Mount.
Completes *The Excursion*.

1814 Publishes *The Excursion*.

1815 Publishes *The White Doe Of Rylstone* and his first collected
edition of poems, with *Preface*.

1817 Coleridge publishes *Biographia Literaria*.

1818 Wordsworth's Tory campaigning for General Election upsets
admirers.

1820	Tours Europe.
1835	Mental breakdown of Dorothy (from which she is never to recover).
1837	Tours France and Italy.
1842	Publishes *The Borderers*.
1843	Succeeds Robert Southey as poet laureate.
1850	April 23: dies at Rydal Mount. July: *The Prelude* (in 14 books) published.
1873	Rev. Grosart reveals the existence of Wordsworth's open *Letter to the Bishop of Llandaff*.

I – Perspective

William Wordsworth is, despite well-founded criticism, the foremost of English Romantic Poets. Leaving aside any prejudice about ageing, creative decline and the award of the Laureateship – putting it into perspective – during his later years he actually wrote such a vast amount of worthless poetry, that the sheer bulk of it pads out the complete edition of his works unnecessarily, exhausting the patience of readers wishing to explore his oeuvre afresh.

Having, as a young man, had his thinking heavily influenced by the events of the French Revolution, Wordsworth would, sadly, succumb, like so many middle-aged people, to a loss of faith in social progress and human equality. Also, Wordsworth having consciously broken away from his eighteenth century poet's Augustan restrictions, his poetry would, in his later years, regress into precisely the highfaluting artificiality that had been anathema to him.

The poet who had once shocked Dr Charles Burney with his poem, 'The Convict' (included in the *Lyrical Ballads* collection of 1798), with its (in Burney's words) 'misplaced commiseration' with the squalid circumstances of an imprisoned criminal, was to write a series of *Sonnets Upon The Punishment of Death* (composed 1839-40 – published December, 1841) eulogising capital punishment as the only tenable method of law enforcement, for certain offenders, in a Christian country. However, for a really gaudy example of all the poetic faults that the poet had condemned as a young man, condensed into one piece of his, one might (briefly) consult 'On The Power Of Sound', written in his late fifties. Before moving on to write about Wordsworth with the reverence that his best poetry emphatically deserves, it is sobering to quote from stanza ten of the last mentioned poem. It lends Wordsworth's unintended hilarity to the tuneful activities of its mythical, and non-mythical, creatures, in the way it postulates their enslavement to the rhythm of the music:

> The pipes of Pan, to shepherds
> Couched in the shadow of Maenalian pines,
> Was passing sweet; the eyeballs of the leopards [!],
> That in high triumph drew the Lord of vines,
> How did they sparkle to the cymbal's clang!

While Fauns and Satyrs beat the ground
In cadence, – and Silenus swang
This way and that, with wild flowers crowned.

Wordsworth's earlier years were his best. Ernest De Selincourt has written, wisely, about 'the obvious truth that what is great in Wordsworth belongs to a single decade (1798-1807)'. During this decade, Wordsworth wrote the best sections of *The Prelude* (which would remain unpublished in its entirety until 1850). This is his long autobiographical poem which, in books 1 and 2, transfigures his childhood recollections with brilliant, visionary poetry. Of the thirteen books that make up the complete version, others recount his unhappiness at Cambridge, his walking tour of the Alps, and his time in France, where he received his first-hand education in republican idealism (and, just as tellingly, in republican practicality).

Throughout these poetic recollections, collectively known as *The Prelude*, the elaboration of Wordsworth's style is largely due to his perpetual effort to squeeze something like an artist's tones and colours out of pen and paper. He adored the chiaroscurism of Rembrandt. The Dutch painter seemed somehow able – with his famous handling of light and shade – to invest worldly scenes with intimations of spiritual reality. In visual terms, it is as if the recalcitrance of Wordsworth's recollections was a stimulus to ever-greater feats of creation:

... The garden lay
Upon a slope surmounted by a plain
Of a small bowling-green; beneath us stood
A grove, with gleams of water through the trees
And over the tree-tops...
... But, ere nightfall,
When in our pinnace we returned at leisure
Over the shadowy lake, and to the beach
Of some small island steered our course with one,
The Minstrel of the Troop, and left him there,
And rowed off gently, while he blew his flute
Alone upon the rock – oh, then, the calm
And dead still water lay upon my mind
Even with a weight of pleasure, and the sky,
Never before so beautiful, sank down
Into my heart, and held me like a dream!

But Wordsworth would, on and off, spend half a century tinkering technically with *The Prelude*. He created, inadvertently, academic employment for generations – what William James referred to as the Phd Industry – with the patience and resources to compare and contrast, in detail, the merits of, say, the 1805 and the 1850 versions.

Lines Written A Few Miles Above Tintern Abbey (1798), from the *Lyrical Ballads* collection, is written in the same style of blank verse as *The Prelude*. Wordsworth has only a pen, yet cannot rest until he has wrung from it a brush's work:

> … I cannot paint
> What then I was. The sounding cataract
> Haunted me like a passion: the tall rock,
> The mountain, and the deep and gloomy wood,
> Their colours and their forms, were then to me
> An appetite.

This poem records his return to a spot on the Wye river, five years after his having first visited it:

> Five years have past: five summers, with the length
> Of five long winters! and again I hear
> These waters, rolling from their mountain-springs
> With a soft inland murmur.

Although in the same place, the poet's feelings are different from those of five years ago. His sister, Dorothy Wordsworth, is a barometer of his own psychological change during his absence:

> …and in thy voice I catch
> The language of my former heart, and read
> My former pleasures in the shooting lights
> Of thy wild eyes. Oh! yet a little while
> May I behold in thee what I was once,
> My dear, dear Sister!

Wordsworth also wrote wonderful ballads. These contained very serious – yet pithily rhyming – exhortations – half-hidden by the apparently not so serious bounding metre – to immerse oneself in the natural world, not the world of books:

Books! 'tis a dull and endless strife:
Come, hear the woodland linnet,
How sweet his music! On my life,
There's more of wisdom in it.

This was not the arcane work of a William Blake, whose personal, religious vision – especially in a post-Enlightenment Europe – of a New Jerusalem, was easily classifiable, and therefore perhaps dismissible as the ravings of a madman. (Blake claimed that he conversed regularly with angels and it was not uncommon for him and his wife to sit, naked, in their garden reading Milton's *Paradise Lost* aloud to each other. So, Blake's contemporary readers, or critics, possessing the fashionable amount of worldly cynicism, would, of course, usually have been predisposed to reject the utterances of such a man.) No, this was the condensed wisdom of a perfectly sane Dalesman who hardheadedly rejected what was not natural – and whether this was the uselessness of scholarly erudition or the insidiousness that he believed too often attended scientistic reasoning, Wordsworth was against all things in whose names men impose restrictions on the happiness of their fellow beings:

No joyless forms shall regulate
Our living calendar:
We from today, my Friend, will date
The opening of the year.

The young Wordsworth leads a passionate and principled existence that he is rebelliously proud to chaunt (as in the following stanza) was not drummed into him, in his boyhood, by some classics-obsessed, crusty old school-master:

One impulse from a vernal wood
Will teach you more of man,
Of moral evil and of good,
Than all the sages can.

It is as disingenuous of Wordsworth to deny the formidable breadth, and depth, of his book-learning as it had been of the great sixteenth century autobiographical essayist, Michel De Montaigne – whose personal library consisted of over two thousand books – to state breezily that 'I could indeed wish to have a more perfect understanding of things, but I do not wish to pay the high price that it costs... and I turn to reading only at such times as I begin to be tired of doing nothing.' The (rarely acknowledged) extent of Wordsworth's book-learning at Hawkshead Grammar School and St. John's College, Cambridge, is discussed at length, in chapters 3 and 5, respectively, of Kenneth R. Johnston's *The Hidden Wordsworth: Poet, Lover, Rebel, Spy*.

Anyhow, whether one says 'in spite of' or 'because of' all Wordsworth's book-learning, the mystic connection of nature and the human soul also permeates the 1802 ode, *Intimations of Immortality From Recollections of Early Childhood*. In this poem, the child's intense (but by no means strained) receptivity to life's initial inrush of sensations is reverentially explained, by the poet, to be something that dulls down with age. Hence,

> Our birth is but a sleep and a forgetting:
> The Soul that rises with us, our life's Star,
> > Hath had elsewhere its setting,
> > And cometh from afar:
> > Not in entire forgetfulness,
> > And not in utter nakedness,
> But trailing clouds of glory do we come
> > From God, who is our home:
> Heaven lies about us in our infancy!
> Shades of the prison-house begin to close
> > Upon the growing Boy,
> But he beholds the light, and whence it flows,
> > He sees it in his joy;
> The Youth, who daily farther from the east
> > Must travel, still is Nature's Priest,
> > And by the vision splendid
> > Is on his way attended;
> At length, the man perceives it die away,
> And fade into the light of common day.

This has kept its spiritual heat, even into the late twentieth century, and can still thaw the iciness out of one's nihilism, or agnosticism, or whatever other pre-millennial chills have motivated even those with the bleakest modern vision. Philip Larkin confessed, in an interview, how he had once been moved by this poem, for a few moments, out of his usual mode of perfectionist pessimism:

Wordsworth was nearly the price of me once. I was driving down the M1 on a Saturday morning; they had this poetry slot on the radio, "Time for Verse". It was a lovely summer morning and someone suddenly started reading the Immortality ode, and I couldn't see for tears. And when you're driving down the middle lane at seventy miles an hour... I don't suppose I'd read that poem for twenty years. It's amazing how effective it was when I was totally unprepared for it...

Other poems, that the reader new to Wordsworth ought first to read, include *Resolution and Independence* (1802): basically, Wordsworth's inspired, and versified, method of beating manic depression; and his sonnet 'Composed Upon Westminster Bridge' (1802), in which the city of London is captured in an early morning state of uncharacteristic repose.

The Preface to the 1802 *Lyrical Ballads* should also be given serious consideration by the Wordsworth initiate. It is still relevant today as a cultural critique, especially when it vents, at length, its author's feelings about the unprecedented proliferation of books and newspapers, and the adverse effects on society of the all too readily available bad literature.

II – The 1790s Pre-Visionary Development

As a twenty-year-old undergraduate, Wordsworth crossed the Alps with his friend, Robert Jones. Wordsworth's decision, in the summer of 1790, to spend three months touring Europe on foot, rather than join a Lakeland reading party to ensure his success in an honours degree at Cambridge (that everyone expected of him) was rebellious and romantic.

He would not graduate with honours. Nor would he take orders immediately after graduating, as his uncle, William Cookson, expected him. The thought of 'vegetating on a paltry curacy' had always repelled him. Yet it was becoming increasingly apparent that this was his only financially comfortable career option. Anyone who cares about English poetry should appreciate the young man's having chosen, or rather, his having created for himself, a much more drastic, and seemingly foolhardy, option. His fledgling romantic sensibilities took off. Had it not been for this flagrant act of disobedience, the different effect upon the whole subsequent progeny of nineteenth century English literature would have been incalculable. This is because, on that 1790 walking tour, Wordsworth acquired what would later become an extremely influential mode of poetic perception, in which the ultimate aim of the writer would be, not to describe nature, but rather, the human mind at work on nature. In other words, Wordsworth did *not* achieve the poetic greatness that is commonly accredited to him by simply responding to sublime natural scenery with turns of phrase inspired to reflect that sublimity. Thomas Gray (1716-1771) had done that fifty years earlier, most notably with his poetic response (though written in prose) to the Chartreuse, on his journey to Geneva, sharing a carriage with Horace Walpole, in 1739:

> In our little journey up the Grande Chartreuse, I do not
> remember to have gone ten paces without an exclamation, that
> there was no restraining: Not a precipice, not a torrent, not a
> cliff, but is pregnant with religion and poetry. There are certain
> scenes that would awe an atheist into belief, without the help of
> other argument.

Wordsworth would look at the celebrated external scene for himself and be disappointed. Gray had said: 'One need not have a very fantastic imagination to see spirits there at noon-day'. But the absence of spirits swarming about in such a way as to set the precipices, torrents and cliffs aglow with their otherworldly refulgence, incited Wordsworth to begin to think differently about the following philosophical problem: What could the real essence of sublimity possibly *be*?

His disappointment, in the face of certain events or states presupposed to induce sublimity, would later surface in Wordsworth's *Prelude* (published in 1850). In the section of *The Prelude* recounting Wordsworth's, and Jones's, first experience of crossing the famous Alps, there is dramatic tension before the young poet's life-changing, character-forming shock of unrewarded physical exertion and deflated spiritual anticipation:

The only track now visible was one
That from the torrent's further brink held forth
Conspicuous invitation to ascend
A lofty mountain. After brief delay
Crossing the unbridged stream, that road we took,
And clomb with eagerness, till anxious fears
Intruded, for we failed to overtake
Our comrades gone before. By fortunate chance,
While every moment added doubt to doubt,
A peasant met us, from whose mouth we learned
That to the spot which had perplexed us first
We must descend, and there should find the road,
Which in the stormy channel of the stream
Lay a few steps, and then along its banks;
And, that our future course, all plain to sight,
Was downwards, with the current of that stream.
Loth to believe what we so grieved to hear,
For still we had hopes that pointed to the clouds,
We questioned him again, and yet again;
But every word that from the peasant's lips
Came in reply, translated by our feelings,
Ended in this, – *that we had crossed the Alps.*

But the thing that Wordsworh discovered here was much, much more unsettling than merely the blankness of the tourist's sight-seeing anticlimax:

Imagination – here the Power so called
Through sad incompetence of human speech,
That awful Power rose from the mind's abyss
Like an unfathered vapour that enwraps,
At once, some lonely traveller…

It suddenly became intensely, and unavoidably, apparent to the young Wordsworth that it was one occupation to create poetry by cobbling a series of visual specifics together as a piece of work describing what he had seen on his travels, but it would be quite another, his having suddenly countenanced the shocking, shapeless vastness of his own psychological depth, to harness *that* (that is, the more important philosophical truth) with words. As he would write, in *The Prelude*, about a decade later (having spent his young manhood reconciling himself to the first-hand evidence of the infinity within, that had so appalled him at the first encounter):

> Hard task to analyse a soul.

As it turned out, Wordsworth would be given the most extraordinary help with this 'Hard task' by one of the most extraordinary men that ever lived.[1] But, in deference to the wisdom and discipline of a chronological approach to the subject of Wordsworth, I will return to this pivotal point later.

In the meantime, however, Wordsworth, in his early twenties, was not yet intellectually equipped to formulate what would later be, in philosophical terms, his corroboratory poetry (*The Prelude*) to Immanuel Kant's seminal idea of the Sublime, situated in the human mind:

> ... A plastic power
> Abode with me; a forming hand, at times
> Rebellious, acting in a devious mood;
> A local spirit of his own, at war
> With general tendency, but, for the most,
> Subservient strictly to external things
> With which it communed. An auxiliar light
> Came from my mind, which on the setting sun
> Bestowed new splendour; the melodious birds,
> The fluttering breezes, fountains that run on
> Murmuring so sweetly in themselves, obeyed
> A like dominion, and the midnight storm
> Grew darker in the presence of my eye:
> Hence my obeisance, my devotion hence
> And hence my transport.

Wordsworth would, for the time being, be isolated from his own truly original source of creativity by his lack of poetic technique. The gulf, between what he was able to articulate, and the feelings that were deep within him impatiently awaiting articulation, was gapingly present – as it is, and remains so for life, in the case of most of all those who have ever tried to bridge it. He would be trapped in the diction, the habits, and the two-dimensionality of eighteenth century poetry, having himself, on that Alpine crossing, peeked over the edge and witnessed the awful, inexorable, personal truth of the psychological abyss:

> Our destiny, our being's heart and home,
> Is with infinitude, and only there...

For the twenty-year-old student, the real experience of 'infinitude' was subject-matter too hot to handle, especially the 'awful Power [that] rose from the mind's abyss'. He would not handle it at all until he had begun to write *The Prelude*, in Goslar, Germany, during the months September, 1798 – February, 1799. Until then, Wordsworth would have to be temporarily thankful, as a poet, for the fact that birds are so melodious, breezes flutter so pleasantly, and fountains

> Murmur.. so sweetly *in themselves*...   [italics added]

It meant that he could get on with describing *this* kind of thing in his tyro poetry, rather than flounder in an inwardly-directed series of abortive attempts at connection with the ultimately real. In short, he had no choice but to put his insight on ice until the time when he would be intellectually equipped to assimilate it into poetry of technical accomplishment and of lasting significance. The rest of this section concerns what he did in the meantime – during a period which it is fitting to call his *pre-visionary* phase.

Descriptive Sketches (1793) is very much in the standard eighteenth century mode. It is a poem by a poet who *knows* what sublimity is but cannot yet fully express it. (Not like the 'Gentleman, who' as Dr. Johnson says, 'knows how to play the bagpipes, but doesn't.') So, in 1793, Wordsworth, the three-dimensional thinker, is condemned, for the time being, to write a two-dimensional poem – that is, a poem about what he has seen on his travels, rather than a poem about what he has thought on his travels.

Samuel Taylor Coleridge (1772-1834), by far Wordsworth's most important intellectual companion, effectively points out, in his *Biographia*

Literaria (1817), that the eighteenth century descriptive mode of poetry was, for the rapidly developing Wordsworth of the 1790s, a kind of contemporary literary cage – the bars of which Wordsworth, even before the full realisation of his talent would transcend it – had the imaginative power to shake from time to time, to vivifying effect. Even when Coleridge quotes from Wordsworth's **Descriptive Sketches** (which, according to Coleridge, 'not seldom.. justified the complaint of obscurity'), he does so with a kind of curatorial veneration.

It was Coleridge, the critic, who singlehandedly romanticised the story of Wordsworth's struggle out of the general mediocrity of his earlier poetry: 'The language was not only peculiar and strong, but at times knotty and contorted, as by its own impatient strength...'. Peerlessly articulate, Coleridge made Wordsworth exist more excitingly in the poetry-reading public's imagination, from 1817 onwards, such was the influence on England's literary-critical climate of **Biographia Literaria**. Coleridge secured, at once, Wordsworth's place at the forefront of English Romantic poetry, and his own place at the forefront of English Romantic criticism. (Incidentally, had it not been for Coleridge's series of lectures which revolutionised the way scholars would think about Shakespeare, regarding, particularly, his psychological insight into every type of human character, it is arguable that English literature would have lacked an intellectual component whose significance was such that, without it, Sigmund Freud could scarcely have set about creating the cultural sensation that he did.) And so it was that, radiant as it became in the warm glow of Coleridge's proprietary pleasure, even Wordsworth's weaker poetry began to command reverence, as the nineteenth century came of age.

In the best of the later Victorian readers and critics – some of whom had just had the Christian stuffing knocked out of them by the implications of Darwinian evolutionary theory – it would become a reverence of almost the Fatima variety. The poet and critic, Matthew Arnold – one of the Christian intellectuals endowed with the courage to admit his probable cousinship with baboons, in the light of Charles Darwin's **Origin Of Species** (1850) – *could* be solaced by Wordsworthian spirituality in a lately godless universe. And the highly intelligent philosopher – whose own work at its best transcended the mental strait jacket of the 'given' philosophy – John Stuart Mill – whose doubt-ridden agnosticism frequently drove him to despair, saw, in Wordsworth's work, 'a medicine for my state of mind'.

*   *   *   *   *

'Tis storm; and hid in mist from hour to hour,
All day the floods a deepening murmour pour;
The sky is veiled, and every cheerful sight:
Dark is the region as with coming night;
And yet what frequent bursts of overpowering light!
Triumphant on the bosom of the storm,
Glances the fire-clad eagle's wheeling form;
Eastward, in long perspective, glittering, shine
The wood-crowned cliffs that o'er the lake recline;
Wide o'er the Alps a hundred streams unfold,
At once to pillars turn'd that flame with gold;
Behind his sail the peasant strives to shun
The West, that burns like one dilated sun,
Where in a mighty crucible expire
The mountains, glowing hot, like coals of fire.

This is a piece, from *Descriptive Sketches*, which Coleridge quotes in his *Biographia Literaria* to champion, in retrospect, the young Wordsworth in his pre-visionary, soon-to-be-England's-greatest-living-bard state. Coleridge was Wordsworth's most eloquent apologist. He still is. In his *Biographia Literaria* (a brilliant, if infuriatingly diffuse, semi-autobiographical, semi-critical extravaganza) he empathises wholeheartedly with the temporary predicament of poetic genius that has not yet attained the maturity, health, and above all, the poise with which it will eventually unfold on the page:

> And it is remarkable how soon genius clears, and purifies itself
> from the faults and errors of its earliest products; faults which,
> in its earliest compositions, are the more obtrusive and
> confluent, because, as heterogeneous elements which had only
> a temporary use, they constitute the very ferment by which
> themselves are carried off.

In this respect, the 1790s was the decade of Wordsworth's important failures, excepting, of course, the *Lyrical Ballads* (1798), which is a collection of the poems of both Wordsworth and Coleridge, poems rightly considered to be the point of departure, for poetry in general, from its eighteenth century cage of Augustan classicality. The second of these important failures is *The Borderers*.

   The Borderers (composed 1795-6 – published 1842) was a play about, at bottom, the reprehensible nature of reason (properly, 'rationalism') when applied with the murderous intent of many contemporary French revolutionaries. In *The Borderers*, Wordsworth has it that the villain is able to persuade the hero that an old blind man has murdered people, and therefore deserves to die. This highly improbable story is the work of a poet who has not yet found his niche. Wordsworth's bitterness against the universal mania for rationalism elicits little more than this piece of turgidly expressed reactionary conservatism. It is a tedious reiteration of the ideology that Edmund Burke (1729-1797), then Britain's foremost conservative theorist, had expressed in his *Reflections on the Revolution in France* (1790). With all its florid imagery, Burke's *Reflections* had impressed its rather blowsily amplified revulsion at political struggle far into the aspiring Wordsworth's psyche, in the early 1790s. Furthermore, Kenneth R. Johnston has, in his lengthy biography, *The Hidden Wordsworth: Poet, Lover, Rebel, Spy* (1998), recorded how Wordsworth attended Parliamentary sessions in London in 1791, in which Burke's reactionary speeches bristled, daily, with classical and literary allusions, 'and Wordsworth's later predilection for alluding to *Paradise Lost* and *Macbeth* when writing about the French Revolution was certainly stimulated by Burke's rhetoric.' Johnston points out that

> On the fateful sixth of May, Burke satirically cast the
> revolutionaries and their English sympathisers as the witches in
> *Macbeth*, full of "Hubble bubble / Toil and trouble," when
> they stirred the pot of social ferment – leaving the hint, for
> those who wished to take it, that Fox was the Macbeth of the
> moment.

Electrified as he was by Burke's writing and public speaking, the young Wordsworth naturally strove to become the author of similarly stimulating utterances. Act 1 of *The Borderers* closes with a short soliloquy from Marmaduke. It illustrates the young Wordsworth seeking his *Burkean/ Macbethean* depiction of evil, and the guilt and madness to which it can give rise:

> Father! – to God himself we cannot give
> A holier name; and, under such a mask,
> To lead a Spirit, spotless as the blessed,
> To that abhorred den of brutish vice! –
> Oswald, the firm foundation of my life
> Is going from under me; these strange discoveries –

Looked at from every point of fear and hope,
Duty, or love – involve, I feel, my ruin.

Hence, *The Borderers* is an unavoidable feature of Wordsworth's developing genius. It was (thankfully) never performed. It is as though, while clearing out his bureau drawer one day, Wordsworth found a clever Burkean harangue denouncing rationalism. Recognising a glint of genius in it, the aspiring writer emptied it into that sarcophagus of a play which Wordsworth scholars are now obliged to examine for evidence of innate, genius-orientated directionality. Well, there *is* evidence of just that, if we can manage to set aside, for a moment, the play's clumpy Gothicism and its touted tortures of the guilty imagination.

In his attempt to write a play, Wordsworth learned how to use the speaking voice. He had, by now (1795), begun to put his trust in the power of the speaking voice to reach the ear of true feeling. Regarding Wordsworth's rapid progress in the direction of the poetic greatness for which he is now fabled, *The Borderers* can, technically, be understood as *the* landmark en route to his most significant discovery (since his 1790 discovery, in the Alps, of the 'awful Power [that] rose from the mind's abyss' about which he had since been capable of articulating very little). He discovered a new verse form and new sympathies for the kind of people thought to be unfit subjects for poetry. Politically, Wordsworth found that he could control and contain the wearying, contrary ideological patterns of his own mind by putting them in the mouths of separate characters. Hence, his unperformable play was a crucial stepping-stone from *Descriptive Sketches* (1793) to *Lyrical Ballads* (1798): from eighteenth century formalism to (Wordsworthian) modernity.

The real popularising strength of Wordsworth, discovered during a period we now ought to consider to have been his provisional career as a playwright (1795-6), and fully exercised with superb results in *Lyrical Ballads*, lies in his ability to enter the minds of characters utterly different from himself. In 'The Mad Mother' (from *Lyrical Ballads*), he assumes, with (as far as eighteenth century poetry is concerned) hitherto unimagined authenticity, the thoughts and feelings of a desolate, mad woman, suckling her infant son. They have been deserted by an unscrupulous man and left in a hopeless predicament. It is true that his love-affair with Annette Vallon, in Blois, 1792, that had led to the birth of his daughter, Caroline, in December, must have turned Wordsworth's later poetic sensibilities towards the subject of desertion. The pathos of 'The Mad Mother' is enriched further in the light of this biographical detail. Wordsworth's guilt at the unavoidable separation (because of the state of war between England and France) was the ingredient in his psyche to flavour his most justly praised poems, of the *Lyrical Ballads* collection, with their influential *Romanticism*, whereas his bookish pursuit of intellectual justification for his political ideology taught him the, in the end, hollowness of, say, William Godwin's uncompromisingly rationalistic polemics: advocating that one's conduct ought not to be influenced at all by one's feelings (such as the feeling of gratitude, dismissed, altogether, as irrational, by Godwin).

Lyrical Ballads is the work of a poet who has left spiritually unprofitable *isms* (including Godwinism) behind. One only needs to spend half an hour reading Godwin's *Enquiry Concerning Political Justice* (1793) to become aware of the fact that it is turgid in the extreme. Wordsworth's collection of poems constitutes a premeditated emergence of feelings through 'those barren leaves' of hidebound intellectualism through which lettered English citizens are trained to be rational, – and artificial.

Wordsworth's various descriptions of female vagrants, victimised by men and society, are imbued with the rich, sad subjectivity of an intellect which has been through the mill of deep emotional trouble. Not since Shakespeare had a writer been able to deploy such psychological insight to show readers how a person in quite different circumstances thinks and feels:

> Suck, little babe, oh suck again!
> It cools my blood, it cools my brain:
> Thy lips, I feel them, baby! They
> Draw from my heart the pain away.
> Oh! press me with thy little hand;
> It loosens something at my chest;
> About that tight and deadly band
> I feel thy little fingers prest.
> The breeze I see is in the tree!
> It comes to cool my babe and me.

If one is ever going to admire Wordsworth, one is going to admire him as the writer of the above lines, from 'The Mad Mother'. It is true that the potential Wordsworth devotee can be put off further reading by writers whose uncritical admiration for the poet frequently leads them into all the gluttony of hyperbole. But let me pinpoint what it is that makes this poetry still worth reading, over two-hundred years after its first publication. For a man to imagine the physicality of breastfeeding, and the mentality of the mother's love for a child who is, in some sense, a replacement for the lost husband, was an extraordinary turn in the development of contemporary literature. Disenfranchised people were suddenly having something representative of their emotional complexities, and subtleties of sadness, with the occasional glimpse of joy, soliloquised for them by a major new poetic force. Wordsworth had still not solved his most important riddle: how to assimilate his 1790s Alps experience, of major philosophical significance, into cliché-free poetry. But this – as he then thought – *ad interim* immersion in his new-fashioned mode of egalitarianism would perhaps secure the sizeable readership required by a sensitive, self-conscious man whose full-time occupation – poetry-writing – required vindication of some sort.

In 'The Mad Mother', the painful nature of breastfeeding an infant when malnourished is, at once strangely and appropriately, mixed with an evocation of primitive maternal pleasure:

> Thy lips, I feel them, baby! They,
> Draw from my heart the pain away.

Even though she has been *wronged*, and is mad, she is still capable of much love for the child and even some flashes of mental clarity. But the bass note of derangement underscores all the poor woman's damaged thought processes. The result is exquisite pathos:

> Thy father cares not for my breast,
> 'Tis thine, sweet baby, there to rest,
> 'Tis all thine own! – and, if its hue
> Be changed, that was so fair to view,
> 'Tis fair enough for thee, my dove!
> My beauty, little child, is flown,
> But thou wilt live with me in love,
> And what if my poor cheek be brown
> 'Tis well for me thou canst not see
> How pale and wan it else would be.

Interesting and useful though it may be to discuss the contemporaneity of the **Lyrical Ballads** as Robert Mayo did in his celebrated essay,[2] this was, in 1798, an entirely new kind of poetry. (Even though it was not quite the philosophically significant poetry with which Wordsworth longed to light up the dim skyline that connects the mess of human thought, and feeling, to its numen.) *Lyrical Ballads* represents a wholly surprising jump out of the mode of nimbly executed, precision-description poetry practised by, say, William Cowper (1731-1800), who, in the following extract from *The Task* (1785) delightfully evokes, with picturesque economy, a panorama of winter-morning detail:

'Tis morning; and the sun, with ruddy orb
Ascending, fires th'horizon: while the clouds,
That crowd away before the driving wind,
More ardent as the disk emerges more,
Resemble most some city in a blaze,
Seen through the leafless wood. His slanting ray
Slides ineffectual down the snowy vale,
And, tinging all with his own rosy hue,
From ev'ry herb and ev'ry spiry blade
Stretches a length of shadow o'er the field.
Mine, spindling into longitude immense...

By 1798, the twenty-eight-year old Wordsworth, having witnessed as a twenty-year old

That awful Power [that] rose from the mind's abyss
Like an unfathered vapour,

is no longer interested in hammering out admirably accurate *translations into poetry* (as Coleridge called the descriptive efforts of the greatest Augustan poet, Alexander Pope) of nature's external sights and sounds. He has, by now, finally *technically* outgrown this poetic two-dimensionality, and operates, though very often with simple language – 'the language of real men' – in accordance with his recently increased sophistication in understanding matters both psychological and political.

'The Idiot Boy' (from the *Lyrical Ballads* collection) is the story of Betty Foy who sends her mongoloid son (Johnny) on an errand

To bring a Doctor from the town,
Or she will die, old Susan Gale.

Susan Gale is Betty's neighbour who (it is confirmed later in the poem) has merely imagined herself to have been sick:

For what she ails they cannot guess.

Betty fatuously seizes the chance (her husband, a woodman, being at work) to make a hero out of her son. It is true that the whole narrative is charmingly backdropped, and soundtracked, by the kinds of things from which one derives foremost pleasure in reading Cowper's poetry:

'Tis eight o'clock, - a clear March night,
The moon is up, - the sky is blue,
The owlet, in the moonlight air,
Shouts from nobody knows where;
He lengthens out his lonely shout,
Halloo! halloo! a long halloo!

But with a very sound instinct Wordsworth had set himself, almost at the outset of his career, to describe rural sights and sounds. The fact that he often did this so simplistically that it seemed, to many critics, pointless and ridiculous, does not in the slightest alter the visionary quality of the target on which his poetic sights were set. There could not have been a better discipline for the pre-visionary poet. Step by step, he left the region of tried and tested eighteenth century observational poetry to attain his proper sphere. His doggedly won power of expressing the baffling entanglement of the observer and the observed world – as he does with greatest success in *The Prelude* – is the fruit of his apprenticeship; the centrepiece, as it were, of his lifelong poetical campaign. However, it would be wrong to celebrate the philosophical power in Wordsworth's poetry without first examining the nature of his power as a poet of incomparable political significance. After all, chronologically speaking, his first footholds into the minds of a mass readership were political ones.

In 'The Idiot Boy', the emotional complexity, and the fact that it resides just as validly in the hearts of the poor as it does in those of the better off, is – because Wordsworth has made it so – poetry's new political commodity. Betty's pride, as she sends her son on his way, briefly becomes, a little later on, irritation at his failure to return ('A little idle sauntering Thing!'), before becoming anxiety, and then finally, terror. Before her motherly expectation, regarding her son's return, deteriorated like this, Betty had affected more neighbourly concern, for the well-being of her sick friend, Susan, than she had actually felt:

And Betty, still at Susan's side,
By this time is not quite so flurried:
Demure with porringer and plate
She sits as if in Susan's fate
Her life and soul were buried.

Importantly though, Wordsworth's tone with Betty is not at all harsh, even when he recounts the fact that the dangerously long absence of Johnny had split the woman's façade and

...so much shocked her,
She quite forgot to send the Doctor,
To comfort poor old Susan Gale.

Nor is the tone at all harsh with Susan for having pretended to be very ill. After all, what kind of readership would expect fun to be made of the affectations of very poor people? An eighteenth century readership was, unhappily, the correct answer. Wordsworth had carved a revolutionary niche for himself so subtly that it could not have been considered treasonably antagonistic even by British reactionary conservatism. In other words, he had found, without being thrown into gaol, or hounded out of the country, a way of criticising the structure of the society in which he lived as having been machinated in accordance with the exigencies of an aristocratic agenda.

Before Wordsworth's politically *levelling* psychological acuity became known (with the appearance, in 1798, of *Lyrical Ballads*), poor people had existed on the pages of English literature only for the satisfied amusement of the better off. *Lyrical Ballads* was consciously aimed at a middle-class readership: indeed, this was the only social group able to afford it. The Wordsworthian agenda involved quietly, and indirectly, informing these readers that those who did not wear fine clothes were just as capable of feeling deeply as those who did. Wordsworth explained precisely this in a letter, accompanying a copy of *Lyrical Ballads*, which he sent, in 1801, to the Whig leader of the Opposition, Charles James Fox.

So, in 'The Idiot Boy', the chimerical series of tragic ends to Johnny's life that (understandably for *any* mother, be she rich or poor) haunts poor Betty is to be imbibed by a large number of middle-class people, because Wordsworth has thought it a worthwhile exercise to bring about this interface:

And Susan now begins to fear
Of sad mischances not a few,
That Johnny may perhaps be drowned;
Or lost, perhaps, and never found;
Which they must both for ever rue.

The nursery-rhyme simplicity affected by the above example is not the result of the poet's condescending attempt to ape the uneducated mannerisms that characterise the story-telling techniques of members of the lower orders. There is a complete absence of the comic tone. So, what is there left for the reader to feel for Susan, as she imagines the horrible possibilities regarding Betty's son's failure to return from his mission, except compassion? Wordsworth corners the reader, emotionally, into humanity. He checkmates the fashionable, middle-class reader into understanding the minds of the very poor, without allowing his writing to descend into sentimentality.

One generation later, Percy Bysshe Shelley's blood would, granted, 'boil with indignation' in his veins, as he would put it, at governmentally masterminded atrocities – such as the Peterloo Massacre, in 1819, when a radical meeting was broken up by a cavalry charge, resulting in some five hundred injuries and eleven deaths – and at fiscal inequality in general. But, in 1798, Wordsworth was calmly administering the re-humanising medicine of fellow-feeling among English citizens without so much as a single benevolent nod in the direction of revolutionary France. Unthinkably, for a Cambridge-educated man in 1798, he *respected* the unlettered citizens of his country. He could hardly have been frog-marched to the dungeon for that. He had to be dealt with by other means.

The arena of literary journalism offered the critical writer with conservative sympathies, and a talent for argument, the political opportunity to publicly belittle Wordsworth's poetry. The hugely influential Scottish literary journalist, Francis Jeffrey, had no hesitation in taking the necessary reactionary steps against what he perceived to be a republican threat from within. As editor of the *Edinburgh Review* from 1802 until 1829, he repeatedly addressed the intelligent English gentleman's conservative nature, urging him not only to avoid wasting valuable reading time with this tiresome Laker's poetry, but also to be very wary of Wordsworth's political insidiousness. Wordsworth – the new voice of the downtrodden people – *celebrated* the tremendous depth of feeling in the common person. He had appeared rather suddenly, and arrogantly, on the cultural scene, peddling poetic wares around which wafted the unmistakable aromas of Liberty, Equality and Brotherhood. And on closer examination, even the charming little lyric poem, 'We Are Seven', about a small girl's failure to comprehend the concept of death, is very radical. Almost embarrassingly uncomplicated to read at first, the poem, like the little girl in it, is bewitchingly simplistic. Imagine a tight-lipped, intelligent conservative reading this poem, in a political atmosphere aflame with fearful gossip about potential revolutionary violence. He would surely feel that the poem was, at bottom, part of a subversive poet's ploy to smuggle some treacherous, republican *joie de vivre* into England's psyche. That is, Wordsworth allows the eight-year-old girl a degree of unchallengeable authority. He is neither patronising nor sentimental, but he seems to imply that the girl, and by further implication her class, possess a brand of wisdom and knowledge which are at once enlightening and unsettling, particularly for the secure, well-educated elite.

Furthermore, Wordsworth has learned to preach at the social class to which he belongs, many members of which have not yet had their feelings of superiority over the lower class challenged significantly by what they have read. The first of Wordsworth's poems in the first (1798) edition of the **Lyrical Ballads** exhorts the middle-class reader to grow out of his inherited superiority complex which, after all, has no foundation in nature. In 'Lines Left upon a Seat in a Yew-tree', aloofness is viewed by the poet as a telltale of stunted spirituality:

> Stranger! henceforth be warned; and know that pride,
> Howe'er disguised in its own majesty,
> Is littleness; that he who feels contempt
> For any living thing, hath faculties
> Which he has never used; that thought with him
> Is in its infancy.

The politically astute William Hazlitt, in **Spirit of the Age**, called Wordsworth's genius 'a levelling genius'. For Jeffrey, a Wordsworth ballad, pregnant with these socially *levelling* implications, is equal in notoriety to any explicitly savage attack made by the American political subversive, Thomas Paine, on hereditary systems of government.

Of course, it is obvious that none of these poems comes anywhere near to advocating a liberal use of the guillotine on aristocratic necks. Nor is it anything other than very mildly combative of Wordsworth to preach against pride, listed, as it is in Christian teaching, as the first of the seven deadly sins. Instead, with infinitely more subtlety, the poems signal a potential sea change regarding the fallacy that the aristocracy has the monopoly on fine sensibilities. It is true that Thomas Gray, in his famous *Elegy Written in a Country Churchyard* (1746), had already suggested that poor people could possibly have had as fine sensibilities as aristocrats, if only the unenviable circumstances of the former had not prevented their cultivating these:

> Let not Ambition mock their useful toil,
> Their homely joys and destiny obscure;
> Nor Grandeur hear, with a disdainful smile,
> The short and simple annals of the poor...
>
> Nor you, ye Proud, impute to these the fault,
> If Mem'ry o'er their tomb no trophies raise,
> Where through the long-drawn aisle and fretted vault
> The pealing anthem swells the note of praise...
>
> Perhaps in this neglected spot is laid
> Some heart once pregnant with celestial fire;
> Hands that the rod of empire might have swayed,
> Or waked to ecstasy the living lyre.
>
> But Knowledge to their eyes her ample page
> Rich with the spoils of time did ne'er unroll;
> Chill Penury repressed their noble rage,
> And froze the genial current of the soul.
>
> Full many a gem of purest ray serene
> The dark unfathomed caves of ocean bear:
> Full many a flower is born to blush unseen
> And waste its sweetness on the desert air.

But Gray's sentiment had been one that defenders of the Establishment had no need whatsoever to worry about: *if only the poor were given the same chance as the rich (which, of course, as every educated person well knows, could never be the case in the real world), then they might be worth something.* For Wordsworth, the poor are full of worth as they are. Wordsworth worked at the atomic level of utmost simplicity. That is to say, he mastered sub-politic laws in a way that bemused and upset the (merely) conventionally equipped conservative rhetoricians of the day.

Lyrical Ballads amounts to such a subtle declaration of equality – or, as J. F. Danby puts it, 'a revolutionary manifesto'[3] – that it must have been difficult for some eminent reactionaries to agree about how to be seen to perceive Wordsworth politically. Could he have been blithely unconcerned about the potentially political implications of his use of 'real language'? Or, with a more straightforwardly malignant sense of purpose than that, was he attempting to facilitate the suggestible reading-public with an incipient sense of shared moral obligation, to be kick-started, at some later stage, into a violent, and coherent, political threat?

In a letter of reply to John Wilson (1785-1854), who was closely associated with *Blackwoods Magazine* under the nom de plume 'Christopher North', and who had criticised 'The Idiot Boy' in a letter dated May, 1802 ('You have described feelings with which I cannot sympathise, and situations in which I take no interest'), Wordsworth refers to the gap between his audience, who can afford books, and his subjects:

> People in our rank in life are perpetually falling into one sad mistake, namely, that of supposing that human nature and the persons they associate with are one and the same thing. Whom do we generally associate with? Gentlemen, persons of fortune, professional men, ladies, persons who can afford to buy, or can easily procure, books of half-a-guinea price, hotpressed and printed upon superfine paper. These persons are, it is true, a part of human nature, but we err lamentably if we suppose them to be fair representatives of the vast mass of human existence. And yet few ever consider books but with reference to their power of pleasing these persons and men of a higher rank; few descend lower, among cottages and fields, and among children.

The last thing conservatives wanted to see, in their England lately beleaguered by pamphlet-happy radicalism, was a cultural icon from the Lake District swaying the sympathies of middle-class citizens, effectively telling them that antinomianism was not the birthright of the aristocrat. Yet this appeared to be precisely what was happening.

Robert Mayo explains that *Lyrical Ballads* did not meet with quite the opprobrium we have perhaps been led to believe:

> The lack of rapport between the *Lyrical Ballads* and the

general audience, which so many writers have thoughtlessly accepted, has been grossly exaggerated… a considerable degree of rapport with some part of the general audience must be presumed if we are to account for Wordsworth's remarkable rise to popularity. His was not merely a *succes d'estime*. The first edition of **Lyrical Ballads** sold well enough that the publisher was willing in less than two years to undertake a contract for two augmented editions.

It is a worthwhile exercise to devote some attention to Mayo's publishing-facts analysis of Wordsworth's impact on the *Zeitgeist*:

The fact is that the **Lyrical Ballads** did not drop hardly noticed into an indifferent and uncomprehending world. Even Wordsworth's hostile critics were willing to admit his early popularity. The first edition, it is true, numbered only 500 copies; the second, of 1800, numbered 750 more of the first volume, 1,000 of the new poems of vol. II. But there were two other agencies at work, providing in their own ways a more extensive circulation of the poems, and helping the emergent Wordsworth to early recognition: the literary *reviews* and *magazines*. The record of the **Lyrical Ballads** in both lends support to the impression that the work was in fairly close touch with its contemporary audience.

Mayo points out that, thanks to the critics and critical publications, Wordsworth's oblique chastisement of the well-off was given much greater exposure than if it had merely involved the selling of a few hundred copies of the **Lyrical Ballads**:

Far from being neglected by the critics, the 1798 volume was widely noticed, and in the larger reviews – the **Critical**, the **Monthly**, the **Analytical**, and the **British Critic** (with circulations totalling about 12,000) – it was given the attention usually accorded to major poetical productions.

Mayo's well-informed survey, of the sheer size of the impact of **Lyrical Ballads** on the English literary landscape, is startling. With genuine insight *and* erudition, Mayo considers the contemporary cultural nexus, and how a cursory acquaintance with it (so lightly worn by so many scholars) limits our comprehension of just how important it was, to a rising star, for his poetry to attract even lukewarm critical analyses:

> The judgments made were not all favorable, but they were
> more sympathetic than otherwise. Several writers signalized
> the appearance of a 'genius'; and, more importantly perhaps,
> all of them reprinted poems in part or full. It is easy to
> overlook the practice in the eighteenth century of printing long
> excerpts from works under review, since the custom today is
> somewhat different. Writers had good reason to complain of
> such piracy, yet they indirectly benefitted too, for it helped to
> acquaint a wide circle of readers with their names and, in part,
> their writings.

Or, in late twentieth century showbiz terminology, 'All publicity is good
publicity.'

Mayo's research has brought to light the fact that 'in the three years
from 1798-1801 eight different poems were thus reprinted in their entirety,
and excerpts of 25 lines or more from six others.' Furthermore,

> The record in the miscellanies is even more formidable, and
> certainly more instrumental in building the reputation of the
> **Lyrical Ballads**, once the volume came within the purview of
> the magazine publishers. In the month after their publication,
> in November 1798, the **Monthly Epitome and Catalogue of
> New Publications** listed the contents of the **Lyrical Ballads**,
> quoted the Advertisement in full, and reprinted Lines Left upon
> a Yew-tree Seat and The Convict...

The point illustrated by this is that Wordsworth's work operated on a scale
compared with which any previous shrill pamphleteering by feisty, more
predictable political underdogs, such as Thomas Paine, would be, at the
deepest level, puny. In other words, if Paine's **Rights of Man** (1791) had
set off alarm bells in conservative heads, Wordsworth's freshly formulated
brand of radicalism was formidable in a much larger, much quieter, simply
more phenomenal way. And, like woman's suffrage or atomic power to
come, it could never be uninvented.

Thousands upon thousands of citizens were devouring this Wordsworthian food for political thought. Could it have been possible that an
unsavoury mass conclusion about the well-off was in the offing? Would
this peculiar new Wordsworthian egalitarianism soon bestride the political
milieu, having first had literary life breathed into it by the mass publicity

of *Lyrical Ballads*? The Establishment must have quaked in its silk stockings.

In 'The Idiot Boy', having undergone a whole night's anguish of threatened disaster, Betty Foy is like any mother who, on finding her beloved child after having lost him, smothers him with affection and, simultaneously, quivers in the knowledge of how much worse things could have turned out:

> And, almost stifled with her bliss,
> A few sad tears does Betty shed.
>
> She kisses o'er and o'er again
> Him whom she loves, her Idiot Boy;
> She's happy here, is happy there,
> She is *uneasy* everywhere;   [italics added]
> Her limbs are all alive with joy.

As for Susan's mysterious illness, no poet but Wordsworth would have accounted for it by amplifying the woman's genuine concern for Betty's son's safety, and, at the same time, being witty (but not smarmy) about her pretence:

> Long time lay Susan lost in thought;
> And many dreadful fears beset her,
> Both for her Messenger and Nurse;
> And, as her mind grew worse and worse,
> Her body – it grew better.

Wordsworth clearly possesses the eighteenth century satirist's ability to expose petty shortcomings, and to lay bare the thought-patterns underneath silly affectations. But his (delicately made) point is that *all* members of civilised humanity have petty shortcomings and affectations. Both rich and poor people have been known to moan and groan, like Susan, in the grip of imagined death-throes. And, in any social group, parental love and pride has been known, occasionally, to foolishly overestimate a son's, or a daughter's, qualities, as Betty Foy does when she sets Johnny upon a horse and waits for him to save the day. Hence, the literary critic, William Hazlitt (1778-1830) wrote of Wordsworth's '*levelling*' genius. When a large, middle-class readership, in late eighteenth century England, is shown that it is, at the fundamental level, *psychologically* the same as very poor people, unprecedented political implications begin to exist in its collective consciousness, and set about subterraneously activating newly sensed affinities. W. H. Auden could not have given Wordsworth due consideration when he claimed, in his poem, 'In Memory of W. B. Yeats' (1939), that 'poetry makes nothing happen'.

So, as evidenced by the appearance of his *Lyrical Ballads*, in 1798, Wordsworth had fully developed a unique voice by peopling his narrative poetry with different characters' voices (as he had attempted to do, in *The Borderers* three years earlier, without success). But there is another *non*-publication from his 1790s development which requires serious consideration concerning Wordsworth's ascent to the poetic plateau he would reach in 1798 (and on which he would operate, politically, by allegory and implication).

His *Open Letter to the Bishop of Llandaff* (1793) was written in reply to the reactionary Bishop Watson's sermon on 'The Wisdom and Goodness of God in having made both Rich and Poor' (from Proverbs xxii. 2). In this letter (incidentally, never to be sent to its addressee by its author), Wordsworth's anger, at Watson's inability to see that the French Revolution was totally necessary and inevitable, is white hot. It was not published until the Rev. Grosart revealed its existence in 1873:

> What! have you so little knowledge of the nature of man as to be ignorant that a time of revolution is not the season of true liberty? Alas, the obstinacy and perversion of man is such that she is too often obliged to borrow the very arms of Despotism to overthrow him, and, in order to reign in peace, must establish herself by violence.

I will make no attempt to forestall the reader's judgement regarding the contradiction of the sentiment expressed in the above with the Burkean sentiment expressed in *The Borderers*. But I will offer the suggestion that Wordsworth was practising his debating skills (having been spellbound, since 1791, by the eloquent, mighty Parliamentary antagonism between Burke and Fox), and found it challenging to advocate a position in which he did not believe. His interest and competence in politics was way below his interest in the craft of *writing*. He was training himself as a writer in order to be mentally equipped, at some later stage, to be able to compose the more important *visionary* poetry which, for the time being (during the 1790s), escaped him. It is possible that, as he did not publish his conservative play, and did not send his republican letter, he was, indeed, merely shadow-boxing on either side of the ideological fence that divided lettered Europe at that time. His 1790s priority was to master the craft of penmanship so that he would have an immense personal worth deserving of the place he would reach when he emerged from his obscurity.

The biographer, Stephen Gill, says that for some reason or other, the republican Wordsworth never acquired a public identity. It is not known for sure why the letter did not reach public notice. Had it done so, it is difficult to imagine how Wordsworth could have escaped being branded a republican in what was a viciously reactionary 1790s England. This, in turn, would surely at least have complicated, if not prevented, the arrival on the English literary scene of his later, greater *Lyrical Ballads*.

Since Thomas Paine's *Rights of Man* (1791) had scandalised conservative England with its eloquent advocacy of revolutionary violence, 1790s literary-political England had become extremely hostile to even the faintest suggestion of Jacobinical sympathies in a writer. Benign allusions to the French Revolution, however tricked up in the most imaginative allegories and implications, could easily be sensed by the receptive antennae of conservatism. Even William Blake (1757-1827) – the most uncompromising radical artist and poet – stopped wearing his red revolutionary bonnet on the streets of London after George III's 1792 proclamation banning 'wicked and seditious writings' had been issued. Paine himself had to suddenly flee from a radical political meeting at which he had been speaking, and was tracked all the way to France by Prime Minister Pitt's spies.

Perhaps Wordsworth was canny enough to realise that his life's literary fulfilment did not lie in *his* participation in the pamphlet wars. Perhaps he perceived, immediately after having written his *Open Letter to the Bishop of Llandaff*, that such utterances merely added up to the barking of a rather commonplace political animal. At any rate, regarding the function of poetic creativity, the question must surely arise, on Wordsworth's ascent (so soon after this) into the upper echelons of English poets: How did he manage to lever himself out of that ordinariness and into the much more intellectually exciting realm of his *Lyrical Ballads*? Well, the deeper, quieter revolution he would spearhead in 1798, with this collection, would require the enormous input from the – as Rupert Christiansen describes him – 'insatiably curious and breathtakingly well-read'[4] Samuel Taylor Coleridge.

III – The Importance of Wordsworth's Relationship with Coleridge

The beginning of the Wordsworth/Coleridge collaboration can be dated to around the 5th June, 1797. Coleridge arrived suddenly at the Racedown house in Dorset, where William and his sister, Dorothy, had been living for the previous eighteen months. A letter written by Dorothy recounts that the first thing that was read when Coleridge came was Wordsworth's new poem 'The Ruined Cottage'. Coleridge then read two acts of his tragedy, *Osorio*. After this, William read his tragedy, *The Borderers*. This is how the friendship began. The two men had admired each other from a distance until then. (They had met only once or twice before then.) But now they took it for granted that each would read his work to the other. This led to the attempted collaboration of *The Rime of the Ancient Mariner* in which Wordsworth suggested the killing of the albatross and even wrote some lines. This, in turn, led to the bigger collaboration of the *Lyrical Ballads*. That intense first year (1797-8) of intellectual and imaginative exchanges between these two poets would come to be known as their *annus mirabilis*.

Although it is important to realise that, in having written *The Borderers* in 1795, Wordsworth had already tapped into poetic powers that were with him before he met Coleridge, the impact of Coleridge's genius on Wordsworth, during their collaborative period, cannot be overestimated. A. S. Byatt puts it succinctly, in *Wordsworth and Coleridge in Their Time*: 'Coleridge made it possible for Wordsworth to communicate, and thus more precisely to formulate, his solitary thoughts. It is arguable that the beneficial effects on Wordsworth were finally more lasting'. Or, as H. W. Garrod (1878-1960) wrote, 'Coleridge.. was one of those men in whose presence it is difficult to be ordinary. He had (with whatever faults) that generosity of temper which rouses others to their proper greatness'. Coleridge was generous to a fault. His claim that the ideas in the Preface to the *Lyrical Ballads* 'arose out of conversation so frequent that, with few exceptions, we could scarcely, either of us, perhaps positively say which started any particular thought' is worth examining, in that no *poem* in *Lyrical Ballads* is really a collaboration.

The first (1798) edition showcases the talents of two individual, up and coming poets. Coleridge's *Rime of the Ancient Mariner* opens the collection with a sustained whirl-blast of otherworldliness (it takes about twenty intense minutes to read); Wordsworth's *Lines Written A Few Miles Above Tintern Abbey* has the final, quietly authoritative, say. Coleridge's *Rime*, in terms of narrative technique, possessed power, compactness and complication that made Wordsworth's narrative voices, in his poems, seem casual by comparison. Its daring images, whether remote or familiar, make it unforgettable. To illustrate this, it is worth quoting one of the Mariner's recollections of being on the ill-starred ship.

> The moving Moon went up the sky,
> And no where did abide:
> Softly she was going up,
> And a star or two beside –
>
> Her beams bemocked the sultry main,
> Like April hoar-frost spread;
> But where the ship's huge shadow lay,
> The charmed water burnt alway
> A still and awful red.
>
> Beyond the shadow of the ship,
> I watched the water-snakes:
> They moved in tracks of shining white,
> And when they reared, the elfish light
> Fell off in hoary flakes.

Or, the following is said to have caused Shelley, on first hearing it, to faint in terror:

> Like one that on a lonesome road
> Doth walk in fear and dread,
> And having once turned round walks on,
> And turns no more his head;
> Because he knows, a frightful fiend
> Doth close behind him tread.

The Rime's flashes of sublimity are frequent. Coleridge deals with precisely the poetic subject-matter which *Wordsworth* has been unable to handle. Coleridge knows about, and has articulated more readily in his *Rime*, that internalised sublimity which Wordsworth would, only later in his *Prelude*, be capable of formulating as:

That awful Power [that] Rose from the mind's abyss
Like an unfathered vapour that enwraps,
At once, some lonely traveller.

During the 1790s, Wordsworth repeatedly put off attempting to articulate the 'infinitude within' that he had discovered in the Alps as a twenty year old. He now found his new friend had beaten him to it. The utter strangeness of *The Rime* is authenticated by the heartfelt pulse of emotion, restrained as it is beneath the sombre magnificence of its style. This modulated surge of life is masterly. Wordsworth *must* have known that Coleridge's poetry was, by a very long way, the most imaginative. Literary contemporaries responded to *The Rime* in ways they never did to Wordsworth's poetry. Shelley chaunted it to himself in Tuscanny. Byron read it when he sailed to Greece for the first time. Charles Lamb was deeply moved by it. Even Hazlitt, usually given to attacking Coleridge rather bitterly in his reviews, said it was the one poem that gave any idea about the extent of Coleridge's genius. The fact that the number of Wordsworth's poems included in the *Lyrical Ballads* far outnumbered Coleridge's, coupled with the fact that, in terms of its capacity to arrest and inundate the imagination, *The Rime* was stealing the show, made the two poets' project a sort of asymmetrical tit for tat. Coleridge would later write about the *Lyrical Ballads* project, generously asserting that

Mr. Wordsworth's industry had proved so much more successful, and the number of his poems so much greater, that my compositions, instead of forming a balance, appeared rather an interpolation of heterogeneous matter.

If one were to change the word 'matter' here, and replace it with '*brilliance*' the statement would be rendered accurate.

Wordsworth rejected *Christabel* when Coleridge offered it for inclusion in *Lyrical Ballads*. *Christabel* (the first – and best – part of which had been written in 1797) has long since been recognised as one of the major works of the Romantic era. Either Wordsworth's jealous prescience took over or his magnanimity deserted him. At any rate, Coleridge, who had been exploring the effects of opium on the creative process, upped his intake for solace. His *Kubla Khan* (also written in 1797) would not find its way into any version of *Lyrical Ballads* either. It would not see the light of day until Byron had urged its author to publish it, almost two decades later, in 1816. Even then, in the prefatory note, Coleridge would express his unwillingness to offer, as a poem, that which he preferred to consider a 'psychological curiosity'.

Quite simply, Coleridge was *used* by Wordsworth. Wordsworth had engineered the political poise of *his Lyrical Ballads*, in 1798. His seminal elevation of the thoughts and feelings of inarticulate, rustic people started a menacing political ripple. In literary-political England, there was a quiet quake which deeply annoyed reactionaries who sensed, more in Wordsworth's poems than in Coleridge's (Coleridge not having given voice to any idiot boys, female vagrants or mad mothers), some ideological mischief at a deeper level than could be effected by any of the republican pamphleteers. This was precisely the literary-political tension which Wordsworth sought to create in order to be able to use it as the cultural electricity, as it were, required to burn his name into the fabric of literary history. Hence, Coleridge, and his attempts to produce ballads in their gnarled antiquity, became redundant. It was, therefore, of paramount importance to the Wordsworthian scheme that *The Rime* assumed a less prominent position in the next (1800) edition of *Lyrical Ballads*. Wordsworth took charge of the publishing arrangements and juggled the collection into what can only be described as a less collaborative-looking format than the 1798 edition. (Wordsworth's name would appear as sole author on the title page of the 1800 edition of *Lyrical Ballads*.) He did this so that *The Rime*'s strange power would not override his own carefully transmitted political message. He did it so that the noiseless, radical high noon, forced so subtly, by *Lyrical Ballads*, into literary-political focus, would be all his. He sensed the shifting of a paradigm and was eager to superintend the process, himself, from the culturally kudos-grabbing, yet politically innocuous, vantage-point of pastoral poetry.

Wordsworth convinced his fellow collaborator of the inappropriateness to the (*Lyrical Ballads*) project of his efforts. Now, this could have been fair enough, but for the fact that he then promptly used many of those very efforts in his *own* project (*The Prelude*), which he began to write in Goslar, Germany, during the months September, 1798 – February, 1799, when Coleridge was away from him learning German in Göttingen University with a view to studying German metaphysics at first hand. For Wordsworth, *The Rime* may have been an outstanding poem, but it was, in the context of the first phase of the Wordsworthian agenda, clutter. It had to be cleared. Fortuitously for Wordsworth, as his businesslike ruthlessness in authorial matters was becoming increasingly apparent, Coleridge was becoming increasingly dependent on opium. Wordsworth would not have too much of a problem in persuading his enfeebled junkie friend that his attempts were inadequate. Sure enough, Coleridge forsook his nest, replete, in a sense with the golden eggs of Coleridgean thought. Coleridge's submission to (or subjugation by) Wordsworth's ego-driven agenda was total. The *Lyrical Ballads* quickly became *Wordsworth's* project. Poetry, just as quickly, became *Wordsworth's* domain. Coleridge willingly retreated from this domain, wholeheartedly genuflecting as he left it all in Wordsworth's hands: 'As to poetry, I have altogether abandoned it, being convinced that I never had the essentials of poetic Genius and that I mistook a strong desire for original power.' For Coleridge, Wordsworth had recently become the only one with 'the essentials of poetic genius'.

Wordsworth was lucky to have such a genius as Coleridge as an acolyte. Of what other creative resource could Wordsworth have availed, had Coleridge (the man who, from 'a very premature age, even before [his] fifteenth year... had bewildered [him]self in metaphysics, and in theological controversy') not been the acquiescent provider of intellectual and imaginative grist to the Wordsworthian mill? One does not need to bewilder oneself in metaphysics when one's metaphysically bewildered, submissive companion constantly hands over, or unquestioningly allows one to take, the fruits of his life's wide reading, and deep thinking, in a spirit of intense devotion. Wordsworth held court. His poetic needs were met, in considerable detail, by his friend.

When Wordsworth planned to set up a small laboratory, with Raisley Calvert, in 1801, for the study of chemistry, there was a characteristically servile flutter of Coleridgean concern and devotion. Coleridge wrote to his friend, Humphry Davy (then a promising young Cornish chemist), for advice on the books and equipment required to make Wordsworth's undertaking with Calvert a success. Coleridge informed Davy that Wordsworth ought – as he was the greatest poet of the age, about to write the world's first, true philosophical poem – to have 'some intellectual pursuit less closely connected with deep passion.' Coleridge was determined to do what he could to facilitate the realisation of Wordsworth's projected long poem, *The Recluse*, about whose philosophical and autobiographical content the former was often loud with adulatory anticipation.

In the wake of such distasteful evidence of Wordsworth's having used Coleridge, and of Coleridge's apparently having allowed this to happen with scarcely a protest, it is something of a relief to consider a more cynical Coleridgean view about his and Wordsworth's *one-way* collaboration. In a letter to Thomas Alsop in 1818, he finally upcasts in the direction of

> those [the Wordsworth family] who have been so well-pleased
> that I should, year after year, flow with a hundred nameless
> rills into *their* main stream, that they could find nothing but
> cold praise and effective discouragement of every attempt of
> mine to roll onward in a distinct current of my own.

Even the devout biographer of Wordsworth, Mary Moorman, says that the above letter is 'not without some justification, in view of Wordsworth's criticisms of *The Ancient Mariner* and his unenthusiastic reception of *Biographia Literaria*'.[5]

The following interpretation of Wordsworth's creative behaviour during his time of friendship with Coleridge, illustrates that Coleridge was, indeed, fully justified in the above complaint. Wordsworth's manipulation of Coleridge demonstrates how inexorably the end (establishing his own name on the short list of immortal poets) justified the means (disproving his friend's valid inclusion on any such list) in the paradoxically businesslike mentality of the foremost of the English Romantic poets. Many of *The Ancient Mariner*'s images appear in Wordsworth's *Prelude*. (Even the earliest version of *The Prelude* was written after Coleridge's ballad.)

There is one uncomfortable, but nevertheless valid, contention as to why Wordsworth denounced *The Rime* while seeming to embrace and preserve its presence in later editions of *Lyrical Ballads*. He wanted (without antagonising Coleridge, his creative resource, out of what had hitherto been a most fortuitous and dependable acquiescence) to *let The Rime slip* from the reading public's imagination. He wanted to do this so that his *Prelude* would avoid any scathing comparisons with *The Rime*. Coleridge's 'big three' (*The Rime*, *Christabel*, and *Kubla Khan*) all had that immediately apparent poetic power which transports the well-off reader, in imagination, from his well-upholstered seat; to ventilate a large number of middle-class reading-rooms with otherworldly blasts of sumptuous fantasy. So, having successfully blocked all of the 'big three' but *The Rime* from reaching public notice, Wordsworth felt that he was not exceeding his remit as he figured out how to set about unspinning his friend's remaining web of dream enchantment. But he failed. *The Rime* did not, as it ought to have done, in accordance with Wordsworth's plan, sink into obscurity, despite its relegation to the middle of the second edition of *Lyrical Ballads*. It had already achieved its grip on imaginations and, to this day, shows no sign of letting go of that grip.

It would have been obvious to *The Rime*'s many admirers – including Lamb, Hazlitt, Byron and Shelley – where *The Prelude*'s most striking imagery originated, had they been given *The Prelude* to read in 1814, rather than the more pedestrian *Excursion*.

The literary-political achievement of *Lyrical Ballads* is indisputable, and this is not an attempt to demote Wordsworth from the major league of Romantic poets. But it is an attempt to examine the widely accepted monumentality of *The Prelude* with the attitude of a mineralogist who has stumbled upon a characteristically Coleridgean specimen of mineral, prevalent in the Wordsworthian monument. There is no getting away from the fact that in Goslar, 1799, Wordsworth wrote much of *The Prelude* with his head freshly charged and brimful with supposedly discarded Coleridgean matter. Meanwhile, back in England, *Lyrical Ballads* was in its first year as public property and food for political thought. Wordsworth peopled his *Prelude* with the very progeny of his collaboration with Coleridge, whose disenfranchisement (as would be demonstrated by the publishing formats of future editions of *Lyrical Ballads*) he would soon ruthlessly mastermind.

The political implications, with which Wordsworth had sought to impress his literary presence upon reactionary England with *his* poems in *Lyrical Ballads*, became *the* important aspect of that collection. Subsequent publishing steps, regarding future editions, would, therefore, necessarily involve the ejection from the collection of Coleridge's otherworldly clutter. Yet Wordsworth wrote the best of his autobiographical poem (*The Prelude*) using much of that clutter. This is poetic genius at its most ruthless. To convince one's collaborator of the inappropriateness to the (*Lyrical Ballads*) project of his efforts, and then, very soon afterwards, use many of those very efforts in another project (of a non-collaborative nature) in his absence, is the stratagem of a predatory poet. The following six points of comparison between *The Rime* and *The Prelude* exemplify this point:

i)   In Book 1 of *The Prelude*, the little boat which the young Wordsworth borrowed one night

> [Left] behind her still, on either side,
> Small circles glittering idly in the moon,
> Until they melted all into one track
> Of sparkling light.

Furthermore, the young Wordsworth's loneliness was attended by the 'stars', the 'grey sky' and the dark mountains. This whole scene is interestingly similar to the lonely (and guilt-laden) plight of the Mariner in Part IV of Coleridge's ballad. The moon, 'And a star or two beside', provide the light by which

> Beyond the shadow of the ship,
> I watched the water-snakes;
> They moved in tracks of shining white,
> And when they reared, the elfish light
> Fell off in hoary flakes.

For both poets, the combination of moonlight and water effects similar visual novelties. Also, both poems' protagonists are guilty: the young Wordsworth of the unauthorised use of a shepherd's skiff; the Mariner, the forbidden shooting of the albatross. (The fact that it was indeed *Wordsworth* who suggested to Coleridge the killing of the albatross by the Mariner does not diminish the motivation for Wordsworth's meticulously organised campaign to subsume *The Rime*. In short, Wordsworth's anxiety is that if he fails to subsume the ballad, it will be *Coleridge's* name, not Wordsworth's, that will ever after be credited with having possessed such imaginative power.)

ii) In Book II of *The Prelude*, the 'weight' of the water and sky, for the young Wordsworth,

> ... sank down
> Into my heart, and held me like a dream!

Compare this with Part IV of *The Rime*:

> ... the sky and the sea, and the sea and the sky
> Lay like a load on my weary eye...

The idea of one's perception of the external scene somehow concretising itself during the process of internalisation, acquiring weight and dimensionality, is an idea that had teased the more lively, and sustained, philosophising out of Coleridge.

iii) The ice imagery in Book 1 of *The Prelude* is equally Coleridgean: the sound of 'The pent-up air, struggling to free itself' interrupts the firelit comfort enjoyed by the young Wordsworth and his brothers in their little cottage. The hideous sound

> Gave out to meadow-grounds and hills a loud
> Protracted yelling, like the noise of wolves
> Howling in troops along the Bothnic main.

Where else could Wordsworth have taken this eerie, icy imagery from, had he not taken it from Part 1 of Coleridge's *Rime*?

> (The ice was here, the ice was there,
> The ice was all around:
> It cracked and growled, and roared and howled,
> Like noises in a swound!)

iv) Wordsworth's recollection, in Book VI of *The Prelude*, of his and his friend Robert Jones's long, nightmarish wait in the Alps for day to break, having just experienced something sublime and terrifying, is Coleridgean:

> … From hour to hour
> We sate and sate, wondering as if the night
> Had been ensnared by witchcraft. On the rock
> At last we stretched our weary limbs for sleep,
> But *could not* sleep…

The image of deeply troubled *stasis* reminds one of the becalmed predicament of Coleridge's Mariner:

> The breathless wilderness of clouds…
> The widely parted hours…

Similarly, the Mariner's ship 'Stuck, nor breath nor motion'. It was

> As idle as a painted ship
> Upon a painted ocean.

v) The 'cry of unknown birds' filled the woods around young Wordsworth in the Alps; the sea around the Mariner was filled with 'slimy things [that] did crawl with legs'. The two poems' protagonists traverse hostile regions whose inhabitants are powerfully present without being described, by either poet, at all specifically. Each poet knows how to trouble the reader, deep down, with the notion that thoroughly nonhuman creatures lurk in the shadows surrounding both the Mariner and the young Wordsworth.

vi) Still on the subject of lurking creatures, and the *frisson* brought about by one's suddenly having to confront unexamined fears, look at the similarity between the Mariner in Part VI of *The Rime*,

> Like one that on a lonesome road
> Doth walk in fear and dread,
> And having once turned round walks on,
> And turns no more his head;
> Because he knows, a frightful fiend
> Doth close behind him tread,

and the young Wordsworth being pursued in Book 1 of *The Prelude*:

> I heard among the solitary hills
> Low breathings coming after me, and sounds
> Of indistinguishable motion, steps
> Almost as silent as the turf they trod.

This comparison is surely made doubly interesting by the fact that, in each of the above 'chases', the protagonists were being admonished, in some opaque way by the natural world, for having abused birds. Wordsworth recalls himself, as a young boy snaring, sometimes having been animated by

> ... a strong desire [that]
> O'erpowered my better reason, and the bird
> Which was the captive of another's toil
> Became my prey...

(Remember that Coleridge's Mariner shot the albatross *himself*.) Could Wordsworth be indirectly admitting here that his tendency to take, for his own use, the results 'of another's toil' has stayed with him into his adult, intellectual life, and more particularly into his poetic relationship with Coleridge? After all, as the above examples demonstrate, many intimations of otherworldliness encased by *The Prelude*'s seamless recollections were first enmeshed by *The Rime*'s more traumatised immediacies.

Wordsworth's attempt, in the publishing world, to quietly annex Coleridge's *Rime*, had it succeeded, would have enabled *The Prelude* to dominate the contemporary cultural terrain without betraying too much intellectual and imaginative debt to Coleridge. The fact that Wordsworth's plan failed is, I believe, *the* reason for his failure to publish *The Prelude* during his lifetime. For one thing, William Hazlitt, a sour man, was particularly sour about Wordsworth's glacial aloofness. (Wordsworth had become cool towards Hazlitt, and remained so for life, after learning of the essayist's having committed a sexually indecent assault on a Cumberland girl in 1803.) Had Wordsworth published *The Prelude*, it would have been exposed to the inevitable critical scrutiny of Hazlitt, who, it is important to remember, was extremely impressed by *The Rime*. Perhaps, for Wordsworth, the thought of the authenticity of his intrinsic poetic power being rendered everlastingly questionable by a wickedly incisive essay (which no doubt would have found its way into *Spirit of the Age*, Hazlitt's collection of essays noted to this day for their perspicacity) was enough to persuade the poet to withhold, in order to protect from the lasting critical stings (of 'the most malevolent creature that ill-luck has ever thrown in my way'), his definitive poetic statement.

Perhaps the finest example of Wordsworth seeing the imaginative results of Coleridge's labour as 'prey' is demonstrated by comparing Coleridge's 'The Nightingale' (written in April, 1798) and Wordsworth's 'There Was A Boy' (composed, again *later*, in November or December, 1798; published 1800, and eventually included in *The Prelude*). 'The Nightingale', included in the first (1798) edition of *Lyrical Ballads*, was, naturally, admired by Wordsworth. He admired it so much, in fact, that he had to *have* it in some way. A few short months later, separated from Coleridge and writing in Goslar, Wordsworth could not restrain himself from availing of Coleridge's poetic exoticism. Coleridge's conversation piece (as he himself called it) evokes how a large number of nightingales

> answer and provoke each other's song,
> With skirmish and capricious passagings,
> And murmurs musical and swift jug jug...

Wordsworth's piece evokes a similar number of birds (*owls*) answering a boy's 'mimic hootings':

... And they would shout
Across the watery vale, and shout again,
Responsive to his call, - with quivering peals,
And long halloos, and screams, and echoes loud
Redoubled and redoubled; concourse wild
Of jocund din!

Wordsworth's piece would appear in the 1800 edition of *Lyrical Ballads*. Already, the more businesslike, and wilful, of the two poets was asserting himself, at once using up some of, and elbowing aside the rest of, the results of Coleridge's poetic labour that didn't make it into *Lyrical Ballads*. In 'There Was A Boy', Wordsworth even punctuates his narrative recollection of birds' musical noise with Coleridge's 'pause of silence'. In Coleridge's 'The Nightingale', the pause is used to prime an explosion of preternatural strangeness over the reader:

What time the moon was lost behind a cloud,
Hath heard a pause of silence; till the moon
Emerging, hath awakened earth and sky
With one sensation, and those wakeful birds
Have all burst forth in choral minstrelsy,
As if some sudden gale had swept at once
A hundred airy harps!

In Wordsworth's 'There Was A Boy', the pause is different in that it occurs after the owls' cacophony, to facilitate – for the poet – a mild sort of psychological implosion:

... a gentle shock of mild surprise
Has carried far into his heart the voice
Of mountain-torrents; or the visible scene
Would enter unawares into his mind
With all its solemn imagery, its rocks,
Its woods, and that uncertain heaven received
Into the bosom of the steady lake.

The burden of these *épingles* is not to contend that Wordsworth is unoriginal and Coleridge is original. Wordsworth's comprehension of how a young boy's mind is unconsciously packed with matter that will unfold before his inward (adult) eye is – especially in the above example – mesmerising. And also, of course, there is the whole political achievement of *Lyrical Ballads* with which (we now understand) Wordsworth acted as a successful agent of social change without having to endure actual Parliamentary frustrations, such as Tory filibustering, and all the other legislative sleights of hand. Rather, it is truer to say that Wordsworth, in pursuit, now, of the philosophically significant poetry he has been incapable of composing since his strange experience in the Alps in 1790, has so very ruthlessly, one may even be tempted to say callously, used such a huge, unacknowledged fund of Coleridgean *details* – all the ideas and turns of poetic phrase – as footholds up to his own literary self-realisation. It is really up to each individual reader whether to admire or despise him for having done so. No wonder Coleridge became so sullen as to inspire the following short piece, composed in 1806, by Wordsworth:

A Complaint

There is a change – and I am poor;
Your Love hath been, nor long ago,
A Fountain at my fond Heart's door,
Whose only business was to flow;
And flow it did; not taking heed
Of its own bounty, or my need.

What happy moments did I count!
Bless'd was I then all bliss above!
Now, for this consecrated Fount
Of murmuring, sparkling, living love,
What have I? shall I dare to tell?
A comfortless, and hidden WELL.

A Well of love – it may be deep –
I trust it is, and never dry:
What matter? if the Waters sleep
In silence and obscurity.
– Such change, and at the very door
Of my fond Heart, hath made me poor.

Apart from Wordsworth's absorption of Coleridge's coruscating poetic clutter – his integration into his own work of some of it, and his dismissal of the rest – Wordsworth was also helped enormously by Coleridge in a practical sense. Coleridge's abandonment of *Christabel* facilitated his seeing the January, 1801 edition of *Lyrical Ballads* through the press. He helped

Wordsworth prepare about forty new poems for the second volume (remember, with just Wordsworth's name on the title page). Coleridge's friend, Humphry Davy, was instructed by Wordsworth to check the punctuation meticulously, and given the authority to make the necessary corrections.

At this point it is important to include a brief résumé on Davy, in order to demonstrate, from a different angle, the calibre of individual Wordsworth had the knack of persuading into his service. Davy (1778-1829) worked as a laboratory assistant in Bristol in 1799. Here, he discovered the respiratory effects of laughing gas (nitrous oxide). He discovered, by electrolysis, the elements sodium and potassium in 1807, and calcium, boron, magnesium, strontium and barium in 1808. In addition, he established that chlorine is an element and proposed that hydrogen is present in all acids. He invented the 'safety lamp' (or 'Davy lamp') for use in mines where methane was present, enabling miners to work in previously unsafe conditions. In 1802 he became professor at the Royal Institution, London. He was elected president of the Royal Society in 1820. Yet late in the year 1800, he spent many hours pouring over another man's manuscripts, polishing, as it were, Wordsworth's (*Lyrical Ballads*) poetry for its second public appearance.

However, on a deeper level of assistance (that is, in an intellectual and imaginative sense), Davy was a crucial part of the scientific ferment that Coleridge sought to ensure would permeate Wordsworth's thinking as he composed his poetry. It did. In 1799, Coleridge participated in a series of experiments, with Davy, at the Bristol Pneumatic Institute. They attempted to ascertain the effect of nitrous oxide on the brain. This produced a series of almost visionary experiences which reveal startling similarities with some of the poetry written by Coleridge and Wordsworth as the result of their cerebral life together. Davy's laboratory notebook contains his account of a nitrous oxide experience, at which Coleridge was present:

> By degrees, as the pleasurable sensations increased, I lost all
> connection with external things. Trains of vivid, visible images
> rapidly passed through my mind and were connected with
> words in such a manner as to produce perceptions perfectly
> novel. I existed in a world of newly connected and newly
> modified ideas. I made great theories. I imagined I had made
> great discoveries. When I was awakened from this semi-
> delirious trance by my colleague.. who took the gas bag from
> my mouth, indignation and pride were my first feelings. My

emotions were enthusiastic, sublime, and for a minute I walked round the laboratory, perfectly regardless of what was said to me. With the most intense belief and prophetic manner, I exclaimed.. 'Nothing exists but thoughts! The whole Universe is composed of impressions, ideas, pleasures, pains.'

The philosophical excitement that between them Coleridge and Davy discovered with such unorthodox experiments found its way into Wordsworth's comprehension of how he could articulate the remembered strangeness of his own childhood. A comparison of Davy's note with Wordsworth's more famous note (written later) to Isabella Fenwick, about the questionable authenticity of external things in the mind of a young boy, would strongly suggest this:

I was often unable to think of external things as having external existence, and I communed with all that I saw as something not apart from, but inherent in, my own immaterial nature. Many times while going to school have I grasped a wall or tree to recall myself from the abyss of idealism to the reality. At that time I was afraid of such processes.

Regarding this, look at the following childhood recollection, from Book 2 of *The Prelude*:

Nor seldom did I lift our cottage latch
Far earlier, and before the vernal thrush
Was audible, among the hills I sate
Alone, upon some jutting eminence
At the first hour of morning, when the Vale
Lay quiet in an utter solitude.
How shall I trace the history, where seek
The origin of what I then have felt?
Oft in those moments such a holy calm
Did overspread my soul, that I forgot bodily eyes, and what I saw
Appear'd like something in myself, a dream,
A prospect in my mind.

Could this have been composed without the scientific ferment first having been stirred up around Wordsworth by Coleridge and Davy? The more than competently evoked conditions of early morning purity, in which 'the Vale / Lay quiet in an utter solitude', lend an air of almost scientific scrupulousness to a poetic recollection. Through the high-powered lens of a unique memory, Wordsworth analyses the 'data' of his childhood's solipsism. But, just as Michael Faraday (1791-1867) would not have discovered the induction of electric currents without having first been shown, by Davy, how to conduct experiments with electromagnetism, so Wordsworth needed to learn from Coleridge how to 'experiment' on his recollected inner-self in order to isolate, for examination, those moments of remembered epiphany. It is just that Wordsworth did not have to jeopardise his health or sanity (like Coleridge). As far as is known, he never sought to make more extravagant those mental processes which had frightened and exalted him so much in his childhood, by inhaling nitrous oxide or imbibing staggering quantities of opium as an adult. And when it became apparent to him, in the late 1790s, that his new friend Coleridge would perform enough of this kind of tightrope-walking over the abyss for both of them, Wordsworth realised that he had found in his friend a creative resource upon whom his reliance would be prerequisite if he were to have any chance of writing the long poem (*The Recluse*) with which he would take his place beside Milton, in the hall of literary achievement.

IV – The Image of the Poet

It is true to say that Wordsworth benefited enormously from the talents and efforts – and in Coleridge's case, the poetic genius – of people around him. However, his *modus vivendi* would be very different from the one he would have had us all know about. The painter, Benjamin Haydon, would greatly help him cut the profile of the solitary genius – the profile which people, for reasons I shall presently examine, tend much to prefer.

Haydon's 1842 portrait of the seventy-two-year-old Wordsworth, as if on Helvellyn, depicts the idealised image that the poet sought to impress (and, to a significant degree, succeeded in doing) upon the minds of future generations; the image of, to borrow one stanza from Shelley's 'To A Skylark',

> … a poet hidden
> In the light of thought,
> Singing hymns unbidden
> Till the world is wrought
> To sympathy with hopes and fears it heeded not.

In Haydon's portrait of Wordsworth, the rough waters far below, and the blackness of the clouds and rocks, garland the flesh tints of the poet's hands and face. Wordsworth's glowing pensiveness, it seems, glows brighter the wetter, windier and lonelier it is. This painting seems to tell us that Wordsworth, the poet, relied exclusively on powers that burned within, while all without (whether the intemperate climate or ubiquitous human folly) he had had to learn 'to bear and to forbear' (as he wrote in 1833). In light of the fact that this is Haydon's painting of Wordsworth *as if* on Helvellyn – not actually there – there is an uncomfortable question to those who still would much prefer to accept with eagerness this portrayal of Wordsworth as the solitary genius: Why is there no equally famous painting of both Wordsworth and Coleridge roving (as Wordsworth tells us they often did, in *The Prelude*'s conclusion) 'Upon smooth Quantock's airy ridge'? After all, it had been during this time that Coleridge,

> in bewitching words, with happy heart,
> Didst.. chaunt the vision of that Ancient Man,
> The bright-eyed Mariner

(helped, of course, by Wordsworth). Marilyn Butler presents a satisfying answer to this question in the introductory chapter of her perceptive critical study of the phenomenon of Romanticism – *Romantics, Rebels and Reactionaries*:

> The first three decades of the nineteenth century saw the emergence of a heightened interest in the personality of the artist, evidenced in the phenomenal spate of biography. The rage for these literary *lives*, copiously illustrated by letters, was part of a passion for documenting the natural world, including the human and social world; it was a manifestation of a scientific curiosity that extended equally to the animal kingdom, to plants and to fossils. But where the poet was the subject, something more than curiosity was conveyed: a taste was beginning to emerge to see the artist *as a hero*, and this perhaps is the symptom of a special need.

Butler mentions the portrait of John Keats, by Joseph Severn, as another example of this phenomenon, in which Keats is portrayed 'as a delicate adolescent obviously destined for another world'. Similarly, Wordsworth has not been the same man, in our century, since posterity in his own deified him. A hero is somehow not as heroic when presented as having contributed merely to *half* of a joint effort. And, as I have explained, Wordsworth made strenuous efforts to impress *his own* name upon the minds of future generations by playing down that of the well-deserving Coleridge.

So, we want to believe what Wordsworth spent much of his energy in his later years persuading us all to believe. A representation of Wordsworth and Coleridge being intensely, and sustainedly, privy to the light of each other's thoughts could hardly be displayed, like Haydon's painting of Wordsworth, in the National Portrait Gallery, London. And the portrait of Coleridge, by Peter Vandyke, which hangs in the same gallery, was painted in 1792, when the poet was just twenty. In complete contrast to Haydon's work, the background is plain. The Coleridge depicted has neither the years that brought Wordsworth's venerable white hair to Haydon's notice, nor the fictitious commotion of dark storminess at a high altitude with which Haydon effected that memorable foil to Wordsworth's glimmering intellectual lineaments. If one were to guess solely from each poet's best known portrait, one would naturally form the impression that, during their years in conversation and collaboration, Coleridge must have been, intellectually and imaginatively, the passenger. The fact that Haydon,

Wordsworth's close friend, knew, and had painted, most of the eminent writers and statesmen of the day, would keep Wordsworth at the forefront of the nation's cultural consciousness. The fact that Haydon had previously included Wordsworth, in the company of intellectually and imaginatively groundbreaking thinkers such as Voltaire and Newton, in his massive painting, *Christ's Entry into Jerusalem*, was designed to fix Wordsworth, alongside those luminaries, in posterity's comprehension of bygone Christendom, as a key shaper of the *Zeitgeist*.

In other words, regarding all this self-publicity, Wordsworth knew exactly what he was doing, and did it well into his old age. When he was over sixty, he inserted the following two lines into his *Prelude*, about the statue of Sir Isaac Newton at Cambridge:

> The marble index of a mind for ever
> Voyaging through strange seas of thought, alone...

Ernest De Selincourt warned, in 1932, that those 'who accept with too much literalness the obvious truth that what is great in Wordsworth belongs to a single decade (1798-1807)' should note the old poet's peerless 'poetic handling', which inadvertently caused him to lapse back into genius from time to time. In the case of the above two lines, the loneliness of the thinking man is succinctly romanticised. That is to say, Wordsworth has made an 'Ancient Mariner' out of Newton with one sentence. This betrays Wordsworth's lust (evidently not dimmed by his age) for immortality which is – and this relates to a large, off-putting truth about Wordsworth – entirely forgetful of any debt to Coleridge.

Wordsworth's single-minded, ruthless, and ultimately, ego-driven pursuit of immortality was as strong in his sixties as it had been in his twenties and thirties when he had had

> ... a daring thought, that *I* might leave   [italics added]
> Some monument behind me which pure hearts
> Should reverence.

In his continual revision of *The Prelude*, even as he uses the intellectual and imaginative results (as demonstrated earlier) 'of another's [Coleridge's] toil', Wordsworth seeks for himself, as the author of a poem with major spiritual/ philosophical aspirations, the aura of aloofness and separateness that, increasingly, as the nineteenth century progressed, was believed by more and more of the reading public to characterise genius. Hence, Wordsworth (as presented in *The Prelude*), unlike Coleridge,

> ... was [as an undergraduate] detached
> Internally from academic cares.

Elizabeth Barrett Browning wrote a powerful sonnet about Haydon's painting of Wordsworth upon Helvellyn. The phrase she coined about Wordsworth taking

> ... here his rightful place as *poet-priest* [italics added]
> By the high altar, singing prayer upon prayer
> To the higher Heavens

has since been at least partly responsible for ascribing, for many, especially nowadays, the rather irritating characteristic of religiosity to Wordsworth's supposed solitariness. It is worth quoting this sonnet in its entirety as it is indicative of the Victorian (Christian) tendency, that has by no means yet been extinguished, to explain creativity as the privilege of certain lucky *individuals'* special relationships with God:

> Wordsworth upon Helvellyn! Let the cloud
> Ebb audibly along the mountain-wind
> Then break against the rock, and show behind
> The lowland valleys floating up to crowd
> The sense with beauty. He with forehead bowed
> And humble-lidded eyes, as one inclined
> Before the sovran thought of his own mind,
> And very meek with inspiration proud,
> Takes here his rightful place as poet-priest
> By the high altar, singing prayer and prayer
> To the high Heavens. A noble vision free
> Our Haydon's hand has flung out from the mist:
> No portrait this, with Academic air!
> This is the poet and his poetry.

Coleridge, on the other hand, had consistently displayed what would come to be perceived as the characteristics of cleverness rather than of genius. As the biographer, Hunter Davies, says of him as a young man, 'Coleridge was gregarious and impetuous, loved parties and social activities, was always with a crowd of friends, rushing from one thing to another.' And

Coleridge's friends were, like Coleridge, 'the sort of smart, clever young men who were in the set which was asked to write those smart, sharp, clever reviews in the magazines.' The absence of the need, in Wordsworth, for this kind of *un*priestlike, *un*visionary stimulation is a notion that serves no purpose for anyone who wishes to understand the real nature of Wordsworth's creativity during his greatest decade (as De Selincourt defined it, and many agree, 1798-1807).

Those of us who like to think of Wordsworth as the lonely wanderer across mountain ranges, and of Coleridge as the talker rather than a doer (as Hazlitt unkindly labelled Coleridge in a nasty essay) should read the following long, but compelling, extract from one of Coleridge's letters, dated August 6th, 1802. In it, Coleridge remembers the preceding day's events in minute detail, and retrospectively analyses his own decision-making in life-threatening circumstances, in almost scientific detachment from the biasing influence of human companionship. The fissure in the rock, that eventually presented a means of escape from his potentially fatal predicament, is perceived by Coleridge to have been an outward sign of the absolute Truth, believed by both he and Wordsworth at that time, that 'Everything has a life of its own' and that 'we are all *one life.*' But, as is often the case with Coleridge, the conviviality of his letter-writing style belies the utter solitude (both in a mental and a physical sense) from which he often returned, without any trace of vaunting (Wordsworthian) misanthropy:

> There is one sort of Gambling, to which I am much addicted...
> – It is this. When I find it convenient to descend from a
> mountain, I am too confident & too indolent to look round
> about & wind about 'till I find a track or other symptom of
> safety; but I wander on, & where it is first *possible* to descend,
> there I go – relying upon fortune for how far down this
> possibility will continue. So it was yesterday afternoon.
> I... found myself cut off from a most sublime Crag-summit...
> I determined to go thither; the first place I came to, that was
> not direct Rock, I slipped down, & went on for a while with
> tolerable ease – but now I came (it was midway down) to a
> smooth perpendicular Rock about 7 feet high – this was
> nothing – I put my hands on the Ledge, & dropped down / in a
> few yards came just such another / I *dropped* that too / and yet
> another...the stretching of the muscle[s] of my hands and
> arms, & the jolt of the Fall on my Feet, put my whole Limbs in

a *Tremble*... I began to suspect that I ought not to go on...and now I had only two more to drop down / to return was impossible – but of these two the first was tremendous / it was twice my own height, & the Ledge at the bottom was [so] exceedingly narrow, that if I dropt down upon it I must of necessity have fallen backwards & of course killed myself... I lay upon my Back to rest myself, & was beginning according to my Custom to laugh at myself for a Madman, when the sight of the Crags above me on each side, & the impetuous Clouds just over them, posting so luridly & so rapidly northward, overawed me / I lay in a state of almost prophetic Trance & Delight - & blessed God aloud, for the powers of Reason & the Will, which remaining no Danger can overpower us!...if this Reality were a Dream, if I were asleep, what agonies had I suffered! what screams! – When the Reason & the Will are away, what remain to us but Darkness & Dimness & a bewildering Shame, and Pain that is utterly Lord over us, or fantastic Pleasure, that draws the Soul along swimming through the air in many shapes, even as a Flight of Starlings in a Wind... I glanced my eye to my left, and observed that the Rock was rent from top to bottom. I measured the breadth of the Rent, and found that there was no danger of my being *wedged* in, so I put my knapsack round to my side, and slipped down as between two walls, without any danger or difficulty. The next Drop brought me down to the Ridge called the How. So I began to descend, when I felt an odd sensation across my whole breast – not pain or itching – and putting my hand on it I found it all bumpy – and on looking saw the whole of my Breast from my Neck – to my Navel, exactly all that my Kamell-hair Breast-shield covers, filled with great red heat-bumps, so thick that no hair could lie between them... startling proof to me of the violent exertions I had made.

Bearing in mind that Coleridge wrote the above in 1802, and that Wordsworth's 1805 **Prelude** subscribes to a similar belief in some sort of pantheistic benevolence, the attentive reader of Wordsworth must surely recognise much of Coleridge's writings, of the late eighteenth and early nineteenth centuries, as a mother lode of information. It is instantly recognisable that there is not the briefest glance of Coleridge's eye on posterity.

Yet Wordsworth concludes the second book of his **Prelude** with an identification of Coleridge with the city (and therefore, it must be said,

with all that is soul-destroying, frivolous and unworthy of the highest kind
of poetry):

> Thou, my Friend! wert rear'd
> In the great City, 'mid far other scenes;
> But we, by different roads at length have gain'd
> The self-same bourne. And for this cause to Thee
> I speak, unapprehensive of contempt,
> The insinuated scoff of coward tongues,
> And all that silent language which so oft
> In conversation betwixt man and man
> Blots from the human countenance all trace
> Of beauty and of love...

The anxiety about Coleridge's health contained in Wordsworth's farewell
to him, as the former set sail for Malta (where he would attempt to beat his
addiction to opium and his general tendency towards despair) is really, at
bottom, anxiety about Coleridge's being able, at some future date, to help
the author of **The Prelude** brush it up to its long-anticipated state of
greatness:

> Fare Thee well!
> Health, and the quiet of a healthful mind
> Attend thee! seeking oft the haunts of men,
> And yet more often living with Thyself,
> And for Thyself, so haply shall thy days
> Be many, and a blessing to mankind.

Regarding posterity's view of the two poets' joint visionary comprehension
of the world, it is useful to look upon the recorded results of their
collaborative years as a piece of embroidered cloth. Wordsworth ensured
the turning of the *right* side of the cloth – with *his* name on it – towards the
gaze of posterity. But Coleridge's inveterate fascination with the *wrong*
side of the cloth ensured that he would come closer to understanding how
the threads of existence had been worked together, at the expense of cutting
the superhuman profile of the septuagenarian mountain-climber atop
Helvellyn. Each poet got what he wanted.

V – The Aesthetics of Fear and Depression in the Lake District

Wordsworth made a business out of the feeling of solitude. Once he got to grips with poetic technicalities, he wrote about solitude with force and acuity unprecedented in the eighteenth century. He did not cultivate thoughts of the kind of idyllic world much celebrated by the classical poets. The use of solitude to this end had, for Wordsworth, become hackneyed. For example, James Thomson's 'Hymn on Solitude' (1729) concludes on the following selective note of renunciation:

> Oh, let me pierce thy [solitude's] secret cell!
> And in thy deep recesses dwell:
> For ever with thy raptures fired,
> For ever from the world retired;
> Nor by a mortal seen, save he
> A Lycidas or Lycon be.

Like William Cowper's does in **The Task**, Thomson's poetic voice yearns, in the standard eighteenth century manner, after what some people nowadays are still inclined to call 'the good life': that is, one expresses one's chief desire to luxuriate inwardly amidst the fruits of one's intellect, and education, without worrying at all about cutting a fashionable profile, but instead living an outward life of rustic frugality. Wordsworth's poetic voice offered such a different view of the whole concept of solitude because he was not simply interested in having it for the sake of displaying the usual eighteenth century self-pleasure. He had an agenda, regarding his solitary imagination, around which he would develop a method of poetic efficiency hitherto undreamed of. His lyric poems of 1798 show his understanding of the often quantum-leaping nature of the human intellect and imagination, and its natural, superiority over the systematic acquisition of useless knowledge promulgated by wrong-headed educationalists: it may be that 'One moment now... give[s] us more / Than years of toiling reason'. And even if one's mind, for some reason or other, fails to 'drink at every pore / The spirit of the season', it is no matter. The spirit of the season *will* permeate the psyche anyway, because internal psychological realities are mysteriously entangled with the external realities of the natural world. In short, the machinery of the mind will always go ahead and develop its own unrelenting and vivifying interplay with nature, with or without its owner's permission.

Even (as Wordsworth would later record in *The Prelude*) a short ramble through leafy countryside 'Would leave behind a dance of images / That shall break in upon [Wordsworth's] sleep for weeks.'

But a nightmare realm will, intermittently, envelop the comprehension of a sensitive child growing up in conditions of prolonged exposure to the natural world. The young Wordsworth appeared to himself to be at the mercy of huge mountain peaks that could chase after him with monstrous strides when he borrowed a little boat for a night-time thrill (in Book 1 of *The Prelude*). The 'huge and mighty forms that do not live / Like living men' are from the same psychological abyss as the 'hatched fears' that would terrorise a young Seamus Heaney[6] a century and a half later.

John Beer has written, in *Wordsworth in Time*, about Wordsworth's having, as a young boy, been 'admonished by forces of nature, acting in conjunction with the innate powers of the mind itself.' The guilty fears of the boy had frightened him into sensory confusion, and subsequently, an involuntary shutting down of his normal psychological configuration:

> There hung a darkness, call it solitude
> Or blank desertion. No familiar shapes
> Remained, no pleasant images of trees,
> Of sea or sky, no colours of green fields...

Normal introspection had been temporarily incapacitated. Wordsworth, the man, would never forget the nameless terror generated by this strange kind of electrified opacity in Wordsworth the boy. With this specific episode in *The Prelude*, one sees how Wordsworth has shifted poetry's focus – from episodes being merely recorded in verse, to a new, energetic poetic voice exploring the mind's living relationships with events in the world. Not only is the focus shifted, it is also sharpened startlingly. What could be more startling than the recollection of the boat's disorientating heaving motion through the water suddenly and undeniably animating the dark, imposing landscape?

> When, from behind that craggy steep till then
> The horizon's bound, a huge peak, black and huge,
> As if with voluntary power instinct
> Upreared its head. I struck and struck again,
> And growing still in stature the grim shape
> Towered up between me and the stars, and still,
> For so it seemed, with purpose of its own

And measured motion like a living thing,
Strode after me.

In this sense, **The Prelude**, despite the, as Alastair Fowler rightly calls
them, 'churchmanly falsifications of experience',[7] shows Wordsworth to
have been an accurate cartographer of the world *as his previous inner-self
had seen it.*

At first, the state of his relationship with his self seems scarcely any
different for the older Wordsworth represented in **Resolution and
Independence**. He may, just as suddenly, be rendered helpless for an
indefinite period by a spanner, thrown from we know not where, into his
spiritual works:

To me that morning did it happen so;
And fears and fancies thick upon me came;
Dim sadness – and blind thoughts, I knew not nor could name.

The adult is not menaced by the blackness as the child was, as recollected
in Book 1 of **The Prelude**. No mountains give chase this time. The less
distinctive gloom of the adult settles uncomfortably on both poet and moors.
It is interesting that up until this moment in the poem, Wordsworth has
enjoyed the kind of visual specifics that make Cowper's **Task** such a
pleasure to read. Little details, such as the way in which the raindrops
enliven the grass, establish proportion and space. Yet the lively landscape
established by *Wordsworth* differs from Cowper's in that Wordsworth's is
designed to be a backdrop in the reader's mind, complementing the poem's
psychological set-piece. Cowper would have been pleased enough with
cleverly recalling the nuances of a hare's hither and thither motion in sunny,
wet conditions:

The hare is running races in her mirth;
And with her feet she from the plashy earth
Raises a mist; that, glittering in the sun,
Runs with her all the way, wherever she doth run.

But Wordsworth does not stop at this. The attainment of this power of
describing is only his stepping-stone towards an examination of *whatever
it is* that emerges as one's *life* from the puzzlingly intermingled phenomena
of the subjective self and the objective world. He tries to make sense of
himself, in order to make sense of the world. The following, from

Coleridge's *Theory of Life*, reflects the Wordsworthian philosophy:

> [Man] has the whole world in counterpoint to him, but he
> contains an entire world within himself. Now, for the first time
> at the apex of the living pyramid, it is Man and Nature, but
> Man himself is a syllepsis, a compendium of Nature – the
> Microcosm!

Nature's powers are active. They require no formal invitation into the eighteenth, or nineteenth, century gentleman's psyche, and never did. In 1798, Wordsworth wrote: 'To her fair works did Nature link / The human soul that through me ran'. Nature gives all sensitive humans who are exposed to her no choice but to reciprocate, as this stanza, from 'Expostulation and Reply' demonstrates:

> The eye it cannot choose but see;
> We cannot bid the ear be still;
> Our bodies feel where'er they be,
> Against or with our will.

To borrow John Beer's phrase, Wordsworth 'persistently dislocates our perceptions from their educated readiness to see the universe as a Newtonian machine'. The mind's living interaction with nature does not require the ability to measure or quantify in any way the mysterious goings on in the natural world which impress receptive humans: 'The birds around me hopped and played, / Their thoughts I cannot measure'.

However, *Resolution and Independence* (1802) is Wordsworth's attempt to face down the unpalatable fact that one's facility for communing with nature in this manner may suddenly, and inexplicably, desert one at any time. From the shabbier purlieus of the poet's psyche, negative thoughts creep forth, eager, it seems, to ambush him as morbid preoccupations, such as 'Solitude, pain of heart, distress, and poverty.' This is dangerous. The thought of young Thomas Chatterton, the writer of spurious medieval verse, who committed suicide at seventeen, needs to be overridden by a fresher current of thoughts and feelings for the poet to elude deepening depression. Rupert Christiansen devotes a whole chapter of his *Romantic Affinities* to an explication of the paralysing disillusionment and subsequent derangement of certain key poets of the Romantic age (1780-1830). In 'Despondency and Madness', Christiansen asks the pertinent questions: 'But what happened when one no longer heard the divine voices? Or when they became confused and contradictory?' Christiansen's account of the German poet, Heinrich von Kleist (1777-1811) is a disturbing one, in that it demonstrates just how easily the thinking person can be spiritually poleaxed. Before he discovered the work of Kant, Kleist had written in an unflinchingly impersonal tone. His contempt for other writers' need of illusion had been limitless. He then learned the unbearable fact, from Kant, that 'We can never be certain that what we call Truth is really Truth, or whether it does not merely appear so to us.' In *Resolution and Independence*, Wordsworth fears the future catatonia of his own soul, to be brought about, perhaps, by psychologically corrosive thoughts that he simply cannot help thinking. If only Wordsworth had had an ally with whom to fend off the inexplicable depression that suddenly assailed him as he walked on the moors. Enter the leech-gatherer. Strangely, this decrepit old man revitalises the poet. Wordsworth is thus, as an adult, capable of imagining and implementing this means of psychological robustness, which he certainly did not possess as a child. Then, when his consciousness had, equally suddenly, and equally inexplicably, become a miserable place for him in which to exist, he had been powerless to do anything about it. He simply had to carry on until the malady had run its course. For example, after recounting the scare with the boat in Book 1 of *The Prelude*, Wordsworth writes

> ... for many days, my brain
> Worked with a dim and undetermined sense
> Of unknown modes of being; o'er my thoughts
> There hung a darkness, call it solitude
> Or blank desertion.

To blindly undergo such uncomfortable psychological processes is the lonely lot of most people who have ever lived. Now however, the adult poet in *Resolution and Independence* is able to lever himself out of the arena of 'despondency and madness' into beneficial spiritual kinship with the solitary leech-gatherer. The 'blank desertion' he had been so hopelessly unable to combat in boyhood has since undergone a sort of evolutionary change in the Wordsworthian universe, whereby it has dropped the characteristics of simple childish terror and acquired the (equally unfortunate) sophistication of adult depression. But at least Wordsworth has got somewhere in his struggle against the malady. And he does not wallow in any of this with one eye on a Romantic readership. He recounts instead that he redoubled his conversational zeal with the leech-gatherer in order to skip deftly out of the deepening psychological quicksand of

> ... hope that is unwilling to be fed;
> Cold, pain, and labour, and all fleshly ills;
> And mighty poets in their misery dead.

Wordsworth is not interested in communicating any desire to flirt with death. Instead, he is busy poetically relating how a man at the nadir of the social scale can assist Wordsworth, the middle-class poet, who has lived his whole life 'in pleasant thought, / As if life's business were a summer mood.' This indicates unparalleled sincerity rather than any Byronic, Shelleyan, or Keatsian posturing. Wordsworth unabashedly acknowledges the superfluities of both wealth and leisure that have enabled him to regularly compose verse, pontificate at great length, and interview the occasional desolate rustic with leisurely solicitude. Yet the manic depression will not go away. It tortures Coleridge, rendered childishly unable, as he has been, by his opium-dependency, to resist its vile, dreamlike inevitability. It troubles Wordsworth, who gives it a sort of metaphorically observable life within a satisfyingly imposed cage of rhyming verse:

> But as it sometimes chanceth, from the might
> Of joy in minds that can no further go,
> As high as we have mounted in our delight
> In our dejection do we sink as low...

One could argue that this poem has been calculated to vaccinate succeeding English poets against the poison of existential nausea. Poets may sink low, thickly beset by fears and fancies, but they need not allow these to win. For Wordsworth, if a leech-gatherer – filthy, wet, lonely, and probably hungry – can speak cheerfully, 'with demeanor kind' (indeed come across as 'stately in the main'), poets should laugh themselves to scorn for having sullenly indulged in excessive self-hatred.

But surely there must be a glibness in this forced use of laughter which could never have ministered to the more profound contempt for illusory perception harboured by Kleist. What is one to do when one feels the maddening untidiness in the undisturbed depths of one's soul? Wordsworth does not try to tidy what he cannot reach. Neither does he allow himself the luxury of excessive anxiety about the fact that not all of his unconsciousness can be summoned for inspection by his consciousness. He *snaps out of it* with an exclamation which would have been anathema to many earnest thinkers: ' "God!", said I, "be my help and stay secure; / I'll think of the Leech-gatherer on the lonely moor!" ' There is something crisp and businesslike about a poet slapping his own wrists in order to prevent further flirtation with unhappiness. Other poets would have *slashed* their wrists. Kleist shot himself in the head with a pistol.

In Book 5 of *The Prelude*, Wordsworth poignantly apprehends his failure to connect spiritually with poetry which once moved him deeply:

> Almost to tears I sometimes could be sad
> To think of, to read over, many a page
> Poems withal of name, which at that time
> Did never fail to entrance me, and are now
> Dead in my eyes, dead as a theatre
> Fresh emptied of spectators.

The theatre metaphor is at once odd and fitting. There is the implication that the act of reading used to people Wordsworth's solitude for him, but his solitude emptied again. The act of reading used to be, for Wordsworth, as Marcel Proust would later describe it in his essay 'On Reading': 'That fertile miracle of a communication effected in solitude.' It is now, however, the barren dreariness of once loved words, phrases and sentences whose radiance has been extinguished and whose meaning has evaporated. What can be done about this? Again, the poet is crisp and businesslike – stalwart, even – about resisting the kinds of unhappiness in whose wakes lesser poets have been tempted to prostrate themselves in theatrically Romantic swounds. In the *Intimations* ode, he decides that it is better to take action against existential nausea, rather than helplessly suffer its action against him. This necessitates obtuseness. He obliges his thoughts and feelings to dance to the rhythm of his forced cheerfulness. He bullies his subjectivity into oneness with the universe. The forcibly chaunted jollity of stanza x echoes the anxious effort of the poet as a human vehicle on his manmade highway to heaven:

> Then sing, ye Birds, sing, sing a joyous song!
> And let the young Lambs bound
> As to the tabor's sound!
> We in thought will join your throng,

Ye that pipe and ye that play,
Ye that through your hearts today
Feel the gladness of the May!

J. R. Hirsch, in his typological study of Romanticism, *Wordsworth and Schelling*, has noted the straining (adult, human) poet's 'shrill repetitiveness' and its inferiority in comparison with the instinctive gaiety of children and animals. The poet may be managing his sensibilities with a little more brutality than he would have wished to use, but at least he *is* managing them. He has decided not to countenance psychological squeamishness. The *Intimations* ode is, therefore, suitably hard-boiled in a world that promised much at first but gradually became known to us as a place full of pain, misery, and above all, loss:

What though the radiance which was once so bright
Be now for ever taken from my sight,
Though nothing can bring back the hour
Of splendour in the grass, of glory in the flower;
We will grieve not, rather find
Strength in what remains behind;
In the primal sympathy
Which having been must ever be;
In the soothing thoughts that spring
Out of human suffering...

Yet the avowal *not* to bewail the spiritual impoverishment that inevitably accompanies one's 'growth' into adulthood could only have been successfully delivered into as many readers' minds as it has been, by the rhapsodic brilliance of the poetry. Wordsworth is, like his 1790s hero, Edmund Burke, not the most rigorous thinker, but blessed with the power of persuasion. Look at how, in *The Prelude*, he thumbnail-sketches the working-day of a man of the Alps:

Pleased with his daily task, or if not pleased,
Contented, from that moment that the dawn
(Ah! surely not without attendant gleams
Of soul-illumination) calls him forth
To industry, by glistenings flung on rocks,
Whose evening shadows lead him to repose.

Wordsworth's most intensely subjective cry, in the above passage, about the reality of the soul, is made from within brackets. This is a clever rhetorical device the poet uses to disarm readers with harsher, more worldly habits of perception (that is, he anticipates, most readers). The above passage, *without* the nine bracketed words, would not have the same emotive appeal. Wordsworth's '(Ah! surely not...)' is a canny plea, on behalf of Wordsworthian mysticism, to non-mystics. It is a mild kind of intellectual coercion which has been shrewdly disguised by the brackets as an optional titbit. The idea is, if the reader has not yet been borne into Wordsworth's way of thinking by the main rhapsodic flights, s/he may still be compelled in parenthesis.

In Book 1 of *The Prelude*, there is a memorable episode where the reader is compelled to envisage the young Wordsworth and his brothers playing card games in their little humble cottage:

> Eager and never weary we pursued
> Our home-amusements by the warm peat-fire
> At evening, when with pencil, and smooth slate
> In square divisions parcelled out and all
> With crosses and with cyphers scribbled o'er,
> We schemed and puzzled, head opposed to head
> In strife too humble to be named in verse:
> Or round the naked table, snow-white deal,
> Cherry or maple, sate in close array,
> And to the combat, Loo or Whist, led on
> A thick-ribbed army; not, as in the world,
> Neglected and ungratefully thrown by
> Even for the very service they had wrought...

The last four lines of the above recollection communicate some bitterness about the world's unerring ability to dupe thousands of young men into military service (not very long after their having played the kind of soldier games the Wordsworths are described in *The Prelude* as having played) with empty promises of honour and glory. This is poetry so much more innovative and heartfelt, as a sort of hopeless protest against entangling oneself in worldly affairs, than any eulogy on solitude by William Cowper or James Thomson. Most of Wordsworth's readers will have played the kind of games he played as a child. He levels with us, winningly, on the subject of 'Strife too humble to be named in verse.' He conspires with us. Wasn't it marvellous playing silly little games, in the cosiness of home, before we were obliged to go forth into the appalling real world! Any adult who has lived and worked among men, and, inevitably, suffered because of having had to do with them, knows that the painless hearthside scene from childhood is something to be yearned after.

Wordsworth also recalls (at the time of the 'Loo and Whist' scene) the fact that he was aware of the outside (real) world's raging frost, freezing rain and the dreadful yellings and howlings effected by the splitting ice on Esthwaite Lake. These 'interrupted oft that eager game' as disembodied sounds which a sensitive, intelligent, developing boy's mind could easily have housed in hellish imaginings. The power in the 'pent up air, struggling to free itself,' and in the 'keen and silent tooth' of the frost, operates mysteriously, in shadowy distance from the pleasantly warm young Wordsworth. The sights and sounds of the 'real' world, dissociated from their familiar fixities by the ravages of the season, naturally become the fodder of this particular boy's omnivorous imagination. The reader 'hears' what s/he knows must be nature at work, even though these workings sound like unseen factions warring at some murky, metaphysical depth. The hideous din, generated, as we rational beings know well enough, by subterranean forces, is invested with the daemonic commotion of John Milton's **Paradise Lost**. Even a glance at Milton's description of the imagined place beyond Lethe, through which Satan's 'flying march' leads his troops, confirms this:

> Beyond this flood a frozen continent
> Lies dark and wild, beat with perpetual storms
> Of whirlwind and dire hail, which on firm land
> Thaws not, but gathers heap, and ruin seems
> Of ancient pile; all else deep snow and ice,
> A gulf profound as that Serbonian bog
> Betwixt Damiata and Mount Casius old
> Where armies whole have sunk; the parching air
> Burns frore [frosty], and cold performs th'effect of fire.
> Thither by harpy-footed Furies haled...

Wordsworth has no need to introduce 'harpy-footed Furies'. The strangeness of extreme weather conditions will suffice. However frightful the noises are that frequently interrupt the hearthside games played by the Wordsworth brothers, *The Prelude*'s focus is on *human*kind. The child's lack of knowledge, about the natural causes of the elemental horrors surrounding the comfortable home, adds a magically remembered subjectivity to the brotherly companionship, strengthened in isolation. The warm micro-climate, where harmless games were played, is recollected by the shrewd adult poet who knows that his empathy with the primitive, family pleasure, of keeping warm and together during a hard winter, will touch the hearts of many generations of readers to come.

These are the kind of recollections with which Wordsworth justifies – to himself at any rate – his living a long life of 'honourable toil' (as a professional poet, rather than as a gentleman-amateur who earns his living in a more socially acceptable role, such as that of a schoolteacher or a curate). But, in order for Wordsworth to maintain the vitality to be able to treat his career as a writer of poetry as just that – a *career* – he must grant circulation to few emotional extremes among his thoughts and feelings. He prefers to work regularly rather than live his life at inspiration's blithe beck and call. He has no desire to face the destabilising gape of 'The unfathomable hell within' which thrills Coleridge with cumulative hysteria in 'The Pains Of Sleep' (1803). In Wordsworth's sober, drugs-free circumstances, his refractory emotional and intellectual elements can more easily be homogenised within his precinct of controllable thought. In a word, Wordsworth's depression is not of the same incorrigibly vile hue as that of opium-eaters like Coleridge, or Thomas De Quincey (whose *Confessions of an English Opium-Eater* alternately glamorises and reviles his addiction).

In Book 12 of *The Prelude*, Wordsworth's recollection of 'A girl, who bore a pitcher on her head / And seemed with difficult steps to force her way / Against the blowing wind,' is a vision of the kind of moment that visits one from time to time, and during which one's life feels as though it had been tipped over and drained of colour and purpose. Although 'It was, in truth, / An ordinary sight', he feels he

> should need
> Colours and words that are unknown to man,
> To paint the visionary dreariness
> Which, while I looked all round for my lost guide,
> Invested moorland waste, and naked pool,
> The beacon crowning the lone eminence,
> The female and her garments vexed and tossed
> By the strong wind.

This is a wonderfully dismal psychological snapshot, but it is a far cry from some of De Quincey's opium 'journeys' through mental regions of incommunicable desolation, during which

> all changes in my dreams were accompanied by deep-seated
> anxiety and funeral melancholy, such as are wholly
> incommunicable by words. I seemed every night to descend –
> not metaphorically, but literally to descend – into chasms and
> sunless abysses, depths below depths, from which it seemed
> hopeless that I could ever re-ascend. Nor did I, by waking, feel
> that I had re-ascended… the state of gloom which attended
> these gorgeous spectacles, amounting at last to utter darkness,
> as of some suicidal despondency, cannot be approached by
> words.

Wordsworth chose to ignore these dangerous, exotic latitudes of creative
exploration. Fresh Cumbrian air and simple food were the fuels guaranteed
not to complicate his high thinking any further. The natural forms of
landscape and vegetation (as opposed to the hallucinogenic architecture
viewed by De Quincey and Coleridge on their frequently induced descents
from normal consciousness) may suddenly kindle whatever is in the eye of
the beholder with wholly surprising, and wholly fresh, spirituality:

> When, in the blessed hours
> Of early love, the loved one at my side,
> I roamed, in daily presence of this scene,
> Upon the naked pool and dreary crags,
> And on the melancholy beacon, fell
> A spirit of pleasure and youth's golden gleam…

The doleful lot of the opium-eater can receive no such impromptu uplift.
For Wordsworth, only as long as addictive narcotic drugs have not
pointlessly enervated him, man *is* mystically capable of victory over
meaninglessness. Wordsworth is often moved to outright celebration of
this:

> Oh! mystery of man, from what a depth
> Proceed thy honours. I am lost, but see
> In simple childhood something of the base
> On which thy greatness stands; but this I feel,
> That *from thyself it comes, that thou must give,*
> *Else never canst receive.*   [italics added]

For the poet most renowned for having celebrated the predominance of the human spirit so persuasively, one thing required frequent mention: the necessity of maintaining one's healthy capacity to withstand the psychological hardships of a heightened consciousness.

VI William and Dorothy

Really! For every literary genius, there is a host of ordinary writers who, on feeling the painful consciousness of their own comparative weeniness, often hale their betters on the flimsiest of pretexts. Tribunals are set up, and old linen is anxiously re-examined with a view to finding new dirt. Then, it may be proclaimed throughout our lettered republic that *he* (in this case, Wordsworth) *is no better than us.*

Ever since Frederick W. Bateson suggested the possibility of incest, in *Wordsworth: A Re-Interpretation* (London: Longmans, Green, 1954), speculation has inevitably accumulated, especially throughout the 1960s, continuing throughout the '70s, '80s and '90s, into a conjectural crescendo. No question concerning the brother's and sister's constant interchange of metaphysical ideas and opinions has the power to intrigue people as much as the following: Did they or did they not have sexual intercourse? Their letters to one another do show a rather intense fraternal devotion, but is there really ever going to be a scholar who can, calmly and reasonably, convince us that it was *incestuous*? Bateson's assertion that crucial passages were expurgated from Dorothy's *Journals*, by someone or other, at a later date, is circumstantial evidence. It is, of course, entirely possible that letters could be discovered, in the future, that render the concept unarguable. However, in the meantime (and indeed, even after any such event of the discovery of direct evidence) it is surely more profitable to examine the nature of Wordsworth's professionalism as a poet, and realise that he absolutely needed Dorothy (whether she was his lover or 'just' his impassioned soul-mate) to help him maintain this.

Stephen Gill points out that, unlike the utterly rebellious Blake, who could not have cared less about the commercial fate of his *Poetical Sketches* (1783), Wordsworth 'cared about his publications, about reviews, about his audience and his public image.' His publications were his way of exposing otherwise spiritually impoverished readers, he thought, to the beneficial glow of his genius. The professionalism his sister helped him to cultivate was necessitated not as much by the tradesman's pressures and incentives as by (for Wordsworth) the spiritual *need* of the reading public. Supreme arrogance such as this did not always make the Wordsworths the darlings of their contemporaries: 'Mr Wordsworth is never interrupted', Mrs Wordsworth once told John Keats as the latter made bold enough to get a word in edgeways. Wordsworth, his sister, and his wife much preferred the participation of people, in any conversation to do with aesthetics, to be *devotional*. One imagines this rather ludicrous VIP status ascribed to a poet flanked by a couple of intellectual bodyguards who also cooked his food, cleaned his house, and prepared, corrected and re-corrected his manuscripts for him. Mrs Nicholson, the old Ambleside postmistress, was often exhorted by William and Dorothy, after closing hours, to find earlier posted manuscripts so that corrections could be made. Could Wordsworth, on his own, have got away with disrupting the spare time of this poor woman, as he did, with Dorothy by his side, every so often? The presence of Dorothy provided him with a vent for the kind of neurotically charged sensibilities that often make fissures in the sanity of lonelier thinkers. After all, he wrote that 'She who dwells with me, whom I have loved / With such communion that no place on earth / Can ever be a solitude to me.' De Selincourt's interpretation of the brother and sister intensity is the appropriate – because intellectual – one:

> [They shared] an affinity of mind and temper that had united
> them instinctively in childhood, and had been strengthened by
> years of intimate companionship. Like Wordsworth in the
> intensity of her emotions, she had always been like him too in
> her power of drawing inspiration from "hiding places ten years
> deep"...

The extremely cold winter of 1798/9, that William and Dorothy spent alone together, in Goslar, was extremely important, in terms of English poetry. They stayed indoors, telling each other about the childhood years, during which circumstances had forced them to live apart. Wordsworth, stunned by the vividness with which the recollected childhood scenes existed for him, having conversed with his sister about them was enabled to think with a freshened imagination. He was emboldened to consider again the Coleridgean idea of the philosophical/autobiographical mode of thinking, prerequisite to the articulation of truly great poetry. The vigour with which Wordsworth wrote, during these winter months, suggests he knew very well that, in terms of his pursuit of literary immortality, he was on to something. The fact that William and Dorothy appeared, to their German neighbours, to be shacked up together, and that the word 'sister', in German, was a euphemism for 'mistress', was, although it may have been embarrassing at the time, entirely unimportant to the whole Wordsworthian apotheosis.

Dorothy's letters are riddled with anxieties about her brother's career. The following is from a letter in which she expresses her worry over her brother's inability to use his talent with the same eye to paying the mortgage as another writer on the contemporary literary scene (the poet, Robert Southey):

> How different [is Wordsworth] from Southey, who can go as
> regularly as clockwork, from history to poetry, from poetry to
> criticism, and soon to biography, or anything else. If their
> minds could spare a little to the other, how much better for
> both!

William's and Dorothy's letters lament, from time to time, the fitful nature of Wordsworth's writing. The fact that Southey could, it seemed, endlessly and effortlessly pull cotton off several different literary reels, increased the Wordsworths' fretfulness. But at least it was a *shared* fretfulness. Coleridge's gifts were, like Wordsworth's, deployed in a lofty sphere, but, unlike Wordsworth, he was lacking in that spirit which is so resourceful in contriving domestic circumstances conducive to one's peace of mind. (Coleridge wrote to Joseph Cottle in 1796 about the increasingly unbridgeable gulf between himself and his wife, and about his anticipated failure to provide for his own children: 'The Future is cloud and thick darkness – Poverty perhaps, and the thin faces of them that want bread looking up to me!') Wordsworth's complaint about 'derangement' rendering even the physical act of writing painful is perhaps the kind of psychological pain that, coupled with the feeling that there really is nobody in whom to confide, would unhinge a person. (As much a twentieth century pain as an eighteenth century one.) It is precisely what happens in Sylvia Plath's ***The Bell Jar*** (1963): a terse account of a sensitive, intelligent and creative person's breakdown in a world that offers little encouragement to the possessor of such qualities.

Wordsworth coped with the psychological pain, proverbially imposed upon the possessors of lofty thoughts, because his women were good to him as a poet. De Selincourt hints that Dorothy sanctioned his marriage for the good of his poetry: 'He must have a wife and family, for she knew no less than he, that "wisdom doth live with children round her knees." ' The career of the poet topped the Wordsworths' priority list. When his brother, John Wordsworth, died at sea in February, 1805, William was suddenly (or so it seemed until he discovered otherwise) bereft of a financial resource which had hitherto prevented the necessity of his having to work rather than be a full-time poet. Mary Moorman explains that, in the light of John's death, Wordsworth had to take stock and 'acknowledge that the brotherly bargain between him and John – that John would work to make money while William would "do something for the world" – was ended, or at least that its conditions were totally altered.'

To support this view that Dorothy's presence in William's life ensured the preservation of his sanity – and therefore of his ability to sustain a long life of 'honourable toil' – compare the Wordsworths' family effort with that of the Neitzsches. Friedrich's sister, Elizabeth Förster-Nietzsche, was the last person who should have been put in charge of him (he was now mad) after his mother died in 1897. Elizabeth had married Bernard Förster, whom Nietzsche despised as a failed schoolmaster and anti-Semite. She doctored her, by now, helpless brother's unpublished notebooks, inserting anti-Semitic ideas and flattering remarks about herself. The intellectual world's recognition of Nietzsche's genius has, of course, been keen and swift. But his moral reputation in a post-Holocaust Europe has had a long, slow recovery. A kind sister, like Dorothy Wordsworth, can make all the difference.

In a letter to Jane Marshall (11th May, 1808), Dorothy offers us a glimpse into her brother's desolation, his having endured a great deal of witheringly reductive criticism, at the hands of Francis Jeffrey (and his **Edinburgh Review**) every time he has published anything since 1802: 'He has no pleasure in publishing – he even detests it – and if it were not that he is *not* over wealthy, he would leave all his works to be published after his death.' In the same year as this was written, Coleridge was in London trying to arrange a publishing deal for Wordsworth's **White Doe Of Rylstone**. Wordsworth's **Poems in Two Volumes** had just been published, and critically savaged, the previous year. So Coleridge and Dorothy both knew that William's resolve to publish a long poem (about two-thousand lines), with which he was far from satisfied, would be shaky. It was. The thought of the inevitable critical barrage got through to him, and he withdrew it from publication. Coleridge felt embarrassed because, at one stroke, all the running about he had been doing in London had been rendered pointless. It is interesting to note what he did next, as a last-ditch effort to persuade William to give the go-ahead. He actually quoted from a beseeching letter of Dorothy's (from another similar episode) in a letter of his own to William. In other words, *Dorothy's* was the ultimate voice of authority for one to invoke, if one was to have any hope of changing William's mind once it had been made up:

> As to the outcry against you I would defy it – what matter, if you get your 100 guineas into your pocket? Besides, it is like as if they had run you down, when it is known you have a poem ready for publishing... And without money what *can* we do? New House! new furniture! Such a large family! Do, dearest William! do pluck up your Courage and overcome your disgust to publishing. It is but a *little trouble* and all will be over and we shall be wealthy and at our ease for one year, at least.

Dorothy is shrewd enough (as is Coleridge for quoting her) to prick the appropriate points of William's conscience and massage the appropriate points of his ego. In the above excerpt, the family's dire financial straits are starkly evoked without the finger of blame being pointed so stiffly at Wordsworth as to antagonise him further into obstinacy. But also, she spins a little confederacy with him against the whole disgusting (but necessary) business of selling one's poems in a literary marketplace where implacable Scottish reviewers are trusted, by silk-pantalooned Etonian readers, to affix fitting values to new works.

Would new, bona fide evidence of, say, regular fraternal frottage in some Grasmere gazebo, really *change* anything that Wordsworth wrote? Of course not. But there would be a huge upsurge of journalistic interest in the Wordsworths. Weekend newspaper supplements would run feature articles, the writers having hurriedly re-deciphered the mystical pages of **The Prelude**. After all, we have had tasty reportage on Mark Twain's erectile dysfunction, Lord Byron's pederasty, and James Joyce's penchant for women's underwear...

VII – The Significance of the 1802 Preface to *Lyrical Ballads*

When composing poetry, Wordsworth shunned sensational subject matter. His much maligned *Excursion* (1814) quietly boasted refinement and contemplation, whereas, contemporaneously, the prolific, and mildly outrageous, Lord Byron zipped along the literary fast lane in a blaze of storytelling flair. The fact that Byron's romances, *The Giaour* (1813), *The Corsair* (1814) and *Lara* (1814), each exploit Sir Walter Scott's repertoire of romance forms, while accentuating the gloomy atmosphere in, say, Scott's *Marmion* (1808), would not bother Byron's huge, devoted readership at all. Byron's poetry remained emotionally and technically uncomplicated in order to entertain a mass readership. (The less complicated the works, the more easily translatable into many different European languages. Hence, of course, Byron's swift ascent to international superstardom.)

Yet Wordsworth had already proved himself to be profound and eloquent in prose as well as in verse, on the subject of the dissemination of (as he saw it) vulgar (and therefore popular) literature. His 1802 Preface to the *Lyrical Ballads* loftily asserted that:

> the human mind is capable of being excited without the
> application of gross and violent stimulants; and he must have a
> very faint perception of its beauty and dignity who does not
> know this, and who does not further know, that one being is
> elevated above another, in proportion as he possesses this
> capability.

There is something very exciting about the fact that *The Excursion* (a critique of which appears in the next section) demonstrates that Wordsworth was still waging his quiet war with the sensation-seeking junta of contemporary literature. It is important not to place too much emphasis on the very well documented concept of Wordsworth's radicalism degenerating into his political acquiescence. The poet's thorough and subtle thinking (as expressed in the Preface), and how he adhered to its conclusions with moral stamina (twelve years later, in *The Excursion*), is not given its due by such a sweeping notion. The Preface effectively signalled resistance against the English literary ethos of mandatory novelty, whose incipience, of course, troubled far fewer than did, say, the (politically more visible) prospect of certain new corn laws. It has since been easy for many critics, whose negativity has originated from precisely the kind of intellectually and imaginatively impoverished nomenclature warned against by Wordsworth's Preface, to glibly ridicule a self-important poet more interested in the contents of his nation's heads than in the contents of its pockets and bellies. He exhorted readers that human beings are capable of thinking without their sensibilities being numbed by frequently repeated shocks of fresh triviality:

> It has therefore appeared to me, that to endeavour to produce
> or enlarge this capability is one of the best services in which, at
> any period a Writer can be engaged; but this service, excellent
> at all times, is especially so at the present day. For a multitude
> of causes, unknown to former times, are now acting with a
> combined force to blunt the discriminating powers of the mind,
> and unfitting it for all voluntary exertion to reduce it to a state
> of almost savage torpor.

Never having been an advocate of the atrocities in the name of the French Revolutionary cause, the author of *The Excursion* (1814) would still, however, be fighting the mental, or cultural, war against the moral degeneracy he perceived as being brought about by the proliferation of shallow, insipid literature. His writing has since retained and renewed its aptness. Many twentieth century literary and academic lions, such as Aldous Huxley and George Steiner, have gathered their intellectual powers around this compellingly pessimistic feeling of the collapse – morally and aesthetically – of western culture. Close inspection of the following, from the Preface, shows a poet with as much mastery of sociological knowledge as he has of psychological knowledge :

> The most effective of these causes are the great national events
> which are daily taking place, and the increasing accumulation
> of men in cities, where the uniformity of occupations produces
> a craving for extraordinary incident, which the rapid
> communication of intelligence hourly gratifies.

Wordsworth's Preface is a vivid portrayal of the slide of cultural evolution toward total philistinism:

> To this tendency of life and manners the literature and
> theatrical exhibitions of the country have conformed
> themselves. The invaluable works of our elder writers... of
> Shakespeare and Milton, are driven into neglect by frantic
> novels, sickly and stupid German tragedies, and deluges of idle
> and extravagant stories in verse.

This particular sentiment has the most direct parallel with the occasional outbursts of some worthy educationalists today, who decry the fact that more and more Humanities undergraduates are learning to deconstruct Australian soap-operas, and less and less are being exposed to the richness and elegance of the language in Shakespeare. Attic rectitude such as this is cried down today, as it was cried down in Wordsworth's time.

There is, throughout the Preface, the mental urgency and the pragmatic flavour of modern philosophy that is not supposed to have come about until Nietzsche boldly stepped out and spoke up:

> When I think upon this degrading thirst after outrageous
> stimulation, I am almost ashamed to have spoken of the feeble
> effort with which I have endeavoured to counteract it.

The above words could easily be those of a character in a Nietzsche work, but they are, in fact, from Wordsworth's Preface. Repugnance at the thought of one's having been a professional weakling, and the incipient feeling of alienation attendant upon one's affirmation to become stronger, are decidedly twentieth century emotions. Yet here was an eighteenth/ nineteenth century poet foreshadowing some of the Nietzschean cries that would later accompany the birth-pangs of the modern world.

Yet, when Wordsworth counteracts this 'thirst', in *The Excursion* – by not pandering to the public's demand for the narcotic, vulgarising literature with which it has unthinkingly allowed itself to be weaned – he is criticised by the radicals for not counteracting conservative *policies*, and by the rest for being just plain dull. The latter could hardly be the case now, given that the idea (first expounded in the Preface) that steered the writing of *The Excursion* clear of the fashionable taste for drama, is the idea that has since inspired other major cultural critiques.

Richard Hoggart's *The Uses of Literacy* (1957) examines how far mass literacy has been exploited to debase standards and behaviour. It is thoroughly concurrent with Wordsworth's seminal insight. Aldous Huxley's *Brave New World* broods over the stealthily imposed uniformity, whose operations Wordsworth had revealed in his Preface. But the total number of Wordsworth's progeny is incalculable. Many hegemonic anxieties vented by writers from George Orwell to Terry Eagleton, could have their descent traced back to that Preface. Any aspiring scourge of received opinion who has not already done so ought to read the Preface for its gadfly survey of England's cultural decline.

Such has been the potency in Wordsworth's idea of literacy being *used* to control – by whichever power – the thoughts of a country's citizens. Ideas about conspiracy – even if expressed with considerably more paranoia and hysteria in the twentieth century – are often anchored, in the history of good ideas, to the (Wordsworthian) common denominator: that a population's intellectual somnambulism, and imaginative paralysis, have been, and are being, *induced*.

VIII – An unwelcome *Excursion*

For two main reasons, it is still quite readily accepted that, by 1814, Wordsworth had ripened into the sort of sociable conservative best lowered safely into his Anglican grave. The first reason is that he had taken on – *horribile dictu!* – a day-job in 1813. Worse, it was as Distributor of Stamps for Westmorland and the Penrith area of Cumberland. That is, he had to oversee the distribution of returns from the taxed, stamped paper used in legal transactions. Shelley lost all respect for Wordsworth. His short poem, 'To Wordsworth' (1814), laments the defection of the once radical Wordsworth who had lived and thought 'Above the blind and battling multitude' in a humble cottage at Grasmere:

> In honoured poverty thy voice did weave
> Songs consecrate to truth and liberty, -
> Deserting these, thou leavest me to grieve,
> Thus having been, that ever thou shouldst cease to be.

The second reason is that Wordsworth published the 'drowsy frowsy' (as Byron goaded), conservative *Excursion*. This poem was mercilessly savaged, most notably by Francis Jeffrey, in the **Edinburgh Review**, for being

> a tissue of moral and devotional ravings, in which innumerable
> changes are rung upon a few very simple and familiar ideas:
> but with such an accompaniment of long words, long
> sentences, and unwieldy phrases, and such a hubbub of
> strained raptures and fantastical sublimities...

It is unnecessary to labour the enormous impact, upon readers (or, more to the point, *potential* readers) of Wordsworth's poetry, made by the sheer force of Jeffrey's argumentative talent – a talent with which the contemplative Wordsworth was ill-equipped to compete in the combative arena of literary journalism. Wordsworth was repeatedly bludgeoned in public by this professionally obtuse reviewer. The critical reputation of *The Excursion* never recovered from the wounds inflicted. It is usual for the modern scholar's admiration of this poem to be anything but excessive, and his or her enthusiasm for its apparently flat effusions to be exceptionally discreet. But these reservations can seem as the too readily dispensed scholarly opinions about what has long become a poem only to be poked at, occasionally, with a scholarly barge-pole. It is time for the modern reader to stop thinking in clichés about *The Excursion*. Much of it is magnificent; not as good as *The Prelude*, for sure, but compare it to anything written by Alfred Lord Tennyson, or Matthew Arnold, in the nineteenth century; or Seamus Heaney, or Ted Hughes, in the twentieth.

In *The Excursion*, Wordsworth devotes frequent, though, necessarily, intermittent attention to symptoms of the incommunicable that may suddenly grip – and then just as suddenly relax their grip on – his soul. As it had been in, say, *Resolution and Independence*, the scene is set (in 'The Wanderer') with everyday, conversation-filling details, and elevated into verse with something of the touch of Cowper:

> Across a bare wide Common I was toiling
> With languid steps that by the slippery turf
> Were baffled; nor could my weak arm disperse
> The host of insects gathering round my face,
> And ever with me as I paced along.

The strangely onomatopoeic effect created by the phrase, 'steps that by the slippery turf / Were baffled', coupled with the inclusion of that outdoor irritation with which everybody is familiar (insects) betrays no diminution of the poet's technical ability. He is still able to entice the reader into his imagination, having put in place the conversational bait. However, what does *The Excursion do* for the reader (that the proponents of its ejection from our minds, like Jeffrey, miss) having courted his advances? There is certainly no diminution, either, in the frequency of attempts, by the poet, to use, in Shelley's terms, 'words which express what they understand not'. Wordsworth is, as ever, assailed by shafts of visionary dreariness:

> … amid the gloom
> Spread by a brotherhood of lofty elms,
> Appeared a roofless Hut; four naked walls
> That stared upon each other!

It is now habitual with Wordsworth to put into practice what he learned from the leech-gatherer's chance presence in 1802: human company can be the antidote to existential nausea. This is why, immediately after the compellingly bleak recollection of the derelict yet, somehow, actively threatening building's walls (the fact that they do *stare* is, if not threatening, certainly disconcerting), he looks round for a human being. One is there. The spirit of inexplicable happiness retreats like a vampire from a sudden, silent beam of morning sunlight. That human, the Wanderer, is Wordsworth's 'tried friend'. Their friendship has withstood certain tests and is valuable. But what of the time before this friendship? Mere words on a page cannot quite reach the original feelings that gravitated the Wanderer towards the young Wordsworth rather than this or that other boy:

> He loved me; from a swarm of rosy boys
> Singled out me, as he in sport would say,
> For my grave looks, too thoughtful for my years.

The narrator recalls that he had been offered the jocular (sporting) reason for the primary cause of this binding friendship. The reader, in turn, is offered only this reason. He may, if possessed of a natural philosophical curiosity that compels him to, enquire: What is the serious reason? Is there one? The reader is free to draw on his or her own recollections concerning those first glances exchanged with a stranger who would later become a close friend. There is no communicable reason why the Wanderer should have singled Wordsworth 'from a swarm of rosy boys', but the poet does manage to express, with picturesque economy, something inexplicable. In real life (rather than in its artistic depiction) the surprisingly intriguing question concerning *why* friendship arises in the first place nearly always dissolves in the ensuing accumulation of familiarity. It does not dissolve here. Wordsworth's intensity seizes the strangeness and retains interest in its original purity. (Remember that the author of **The Excursion** is widely supposed to have become a poet of little or no consequence.) The strangeness is not adulterated eventually into a sort of mincemeat of more ordinary recollections, as it would have been in the poetry of William Cowper. The obscurity of the reason – indeed, the sheer *metaphysicality* of the reason – for the Wanderer's wish to befriend the young Wordsworth, makes a little pucker on the narrative's apparent ordinariness, to which the more imaginative reader may sense the natural attachment of a sort of nozzle effecting a direct link with an unworldly, mysterious and awe-inspiring sphere of Truth. Its presence, uniquely, exposes the familiar temporality, in and around the commonplace (Cowper-esque) details, to frequent streams of incommunicability, giving those details a sort of alienated significance (not to mention a much longer life in the imagination of the properly attentive reader) – details which, in the hands of lesser poets, would remain commonplace and become stale.

It is unfair to lambast Wordsworth (as Jeffrey does) for gathering the forces of his imagination on the same battlefield and against the same enemy as he did in his earlier poetry. After all, the long war, against the sort of meaninglessness which unhealthily litters the lives of thinking beings, is not over. Jeffrey says he 'cannot help thinking that [Wordsworth's valuable insights] might have been better enforced with less parade and prolixity.' Yet there is the sense in 'The Wanderer' that Wordsworth has organised his imaginative powers in a line that inches its way along the top stratum of his field of recollections, seeking some chink or fault to reveal lower strata, the glimpse of which, he knows, will electrify him into communicating more than just deliciously vague confidences. In other words, the methodical (and therefore, for Jeffrey, drab) Wordsworthian system is actually essential if the spiritual insights sought after are to be won.

The Wanderer told Wordsworth that he grew to love 'Tempestuous nights – the conflict and the sounds / That live in darkness.' The disquieting turbulence of his untrammelled imagination eventually drove the Wanderer to attempt to ballast his soul with a self-imposed, regular application to the laws of science:

> From his intellect
> And from the stillness of abstracted thought
> He asked repose; and, failing oft to win
> The peace required, he scanned the laws of light...

Presumably, the Wanderer studied the works of Newton 'Amid the roar of torrents'. The image of a youth, focusing his attention on a text like Newton's totally scientific, totally rational *Opticks*, whilst surrounded by the deafening noise of mountain waters, is powerful. It is a novel way of implying a message that Wordsworth has, admittedly, conveyed before, but knows is important enough to be conveyed again: *The answers to life's riddles are not necessarily to be found in books.* The lyric poetry of 1798 had exhorted the human spirit away from 'those barren leaves' of learned books. Sixteen years later, Wordsworth has not hoodwinked himself out of his intensely radical belief (circa 1798) in 'Spontaneous wisdom breathed by health, / Truth breathed by cheerfulness.' The following, from *The Excursion*, illustrates this:

> ... Strongest minds
> Are often those of whom the noisy world
> Hears least; else surely this Man had not left
> His graces unrevealed and unproclaimed.
> But, as the mind was filled with inward light,
> So not without distinction had he lived...

The manner in which the uncultivated intelligence of the Wanderer is narrated here is unforced and beautiful. Wordsworth's poetic genius, though, as Jeffrey would argue, tied to the unforgivably uninspired treadmill of certain fixed ideas, had been implanted, in his childhood, with feelings which slowly and imperceptibly rooted themselves there. They now tower in *The Excursion* with a *lived through*, organically grown majesty.

In the first book of *The Excursion*, the beauty of the natural world dances around, and beyond the reach of, the downturned head of the academic slave. The young Wanderer is unable to hear the sound the pages make as he turns them

> Amid the roar of torrents, where they send
> From hollow clefts up to the clearer air
> A cloud of mist, that smitten by the sun
> Varies its rainbow hues.

Had he lifted up his head, the young Wanderer would have seen sunlight and water, vital to life on Earth, effecting the constant interplay of light and shade, and subtle shifts in the complexion of the mist-bow. The scientific analyses he had forced his mind to adopt as mental instruments for spiritual direction, were emphatically flouted, paces away. Yet he was unable to see nature's stunning, inexplicable visual accompaniment to her water's roar that, ironically, deafened him as he fastened his eyesight on the silent pages (the 'barren leaves'). Wordsworth manages to communicate the tension and conflict between learning from books and learning from life. Reconciliation between the two eludes many, many human beings: 'But vainly thus, / And vainly by all other means, he strove / To mitigate the fever of his heart'. Something major, embedded in, and troubling the modern human spirit, is having its mechanism traced by the poet here. An attempt to define what are, really, the goings-on at unplumbed psychological depths, in which the Wanderer's malady is rooted, lends the poem an aura of hardihood and self-sufficiency. Not bad for a poet writing before the advent of Psychology as a subject, with its library of empirical and academic explanations and terminology.

So, to return again to the beginning of *The Excursion*, the reader has been taken for a walk, by Wordsworth, to meet his friend. The first layer of externality has been evoked with, as mentioned earlier, narrative craft in the manner of Cowper. Then, the reader, if so inclined, may experience the ventilation of the temporal by the eternal, via specific strangenesses that puncture and pucker the narrative's ordinariness. The reader is shown how the Wanderer's oral education developed in him that quick clear-sightedness, which, for Wordsworth, is his most valuable personal quality. Wordsworth, profoundly interested in the origin of that personal quality, has discovered that the importance of the tradition of storytelling cannot be overestimated. Currents of unfamiliarity healthily ruffled the Wanderer's growing mind in its enjoyment of stories, and gave the otherwise workaday individual the imaginative vitality to maintain a principled existence:

> ... many a tale
> Traditionary round the mountains hung,
> And many a legend, peopling the dark woods,
> Nourished Imagination in her growth,
> And gave the Mind that apprehensive power
> By which she is made quick to recognise
> The moral properties and scope of things.

The younger Wanderer, naturally, 'had small need of books', due to the traditional abundance of tales and people willing to tell them. The part of his mind that housed his native wit would treat his later, acquired, interest in books as an invasion and an agitation:

> ... books that explain
> The purer elements of truth involved
> In lines and numbers, and, by charm severe,
> (Especially perceived where nature droops
> And feeling is suppressed) preserve the mind
> Busy in solitude and poverty.

Book-learned erudition and untrammelled, native wit were bedfellows whose uneasiness, together in the young Wanderer's mind, prevented him from pursuing the schoolteaching career expected of him:

> Urged by his Mother, he essayed to teach
> A village-school – but wandering thoughts were then
> A misery to him; and the Youth resigned
> A task he was unable to perform.

This poetry is very important because it illuminates a direct link between the recesses of the modern human soul – accessible only to the eye of genius – and the sort of achievement or failure that is clearly visible, even to unimaginative eyes.

One of the twentieth century's major Wordsworth scholars, John Beer, has admired the way in which Wordsworth's poetry accommodates the abrasive coexistence of unarguable external appearances and life-shaping psychological realities:

> Some writers have been intent to write out of their own
> emotions; others have bent their art towards a faithful
> rendering of the objective world; Wordsworth... was always
> most aroused at the points where the two modes met and
> challenged one another's existence, for then his powers of
> passionate utterance and calm, appraising intellect were both
> potently engaged.

No contemporary critic of Wordsworth ever said anything like this. This is because the kind of psychological enlightenment, whose climate was necessary for the cultivation of such a stimulating critical analysis, would not come about until Freud's work had changed the way people thought about human nature.

Wordsworth's receptivity, to how important the primitive processes of a human being's inner universe are to external life, is ahead of its time. The Wanderer is, rather disconcertingly, animated by mental phenomena not yet described or explained by anybody. These (in Wordsworth's time, nameless) phenomena are always at odds with each other and so they continually re-concoct the individual's motivation for his next move in the external world. In *The Excursion*, the external fact that 'the Youth resigned / A task he was unable to perform' was just the visible outcome (visible to anyone) of the psychological struggle that unsettled the young Wanderer's developing soul. Yet it was probably the only one of any interest to his mother (no doubt ingenuously eager that her son got on in life). Wordsworth draws on his own former emotions. The fact that they are his *own* emotions accounts for his power of 'passionate utterance', ostensibly on the Wanderer's behalf. The fact that they are also his *former* emotions, and that, as elsewhere in his poetry, he treats his former self as if it were not him, accounts for the 'calm, appraising intellect.' There had been a time when he too 'was unable to perform' the career (in the church) expected of him. Yet it was not that he had been afraid of doing a proper day's work. Like those of the Wanderer, his mental needs had differed from those of his rustic contemporaries. He knew that he had something significant to say about the human condition. The poet, therefore, appreciates the Wanderer's high grade of quiet courage. It is a quality a poet should posses in abundance in order to heal quickly the cuts from barbed reviews.

It is almost as if, when Wordsworth wrote **The Excursion**, he was pre-empting all the unprecedented critical hostility that would be received by the poem.

Skilful, if at times harsh, literary journalism, of the variety practised by Jeffrey, informed those keen to protect their reading hours from sub-standard literature. It helped them decide what to include in, and leave out of, the next month's select reading list. Wordsworth's work, including **The Excursion**, had the temerity to inform the reading public of its inclusion in the next century's reading list.

IX – Later works

Shelley's anxiety to identify publicly what breed of political animal he is contrasts with Wordsworth's resolve to conceal *his* definitive statement on that matter (*The Prelude*) for the rest of his life. However, in the meantime, the public Wordsworth does his duty as a poet. He entertains and, much to Shelley's annoyance, he instructs, in the literary arena. Perhaps an intuitive knowledge of *The Prelude*'s posthumous kudos made his gusto – often evident in the more conservative Wordsworth, as will presently be demonstrated – possible as he penned what were, in effect, contractually obliging compositions.

His 'Ode To Lycoris' (published in 1820) is a smoothly textured, wonderfully patronising way of replying, indirectly, of course, to an angry young poet like Shelley, who sees emotional eruption as the indispensable incitement to any genuinely political poem. Wordsworth suggests that such intensity is now old-fashioned: 'An age hath been when Earth was proud / Of lustre too intense / To be sustained'. At first, this appears to be a self-effacing poem. But importantly, it is only Wordsworth's earlier 'radical' self that is being effaced: a voracious entity that he had, as a younger writer, privately invoked, in a decade (the 1790s) with a surplus of political food for thought. Shelley, on the other hand, has not outgrown the melancholic disposition that Wordsworth had already recorded six years earlier (in *The Excursion*) as having made his younger self susceptible to ill-starred political zealotry: 'My heart rebounded; / My melancholy voice the [French Revolutionary] chorus joined.' Now, in 1820, in 'Ode To Lycoris', Wordsworth pokes gentle, empathetic fun at anyone who has yet to outgrow their melancholic disposition that makes them similarly seducible:

> In youth we love the darksome lawn
> Brushed by the owlet's wing;
> Then, Twilight is preferred to Dawn,
> And Autumn to the Spring.
> Sad fancies do we then affect,
> In luxury of disrespect
> To our own prodigal excess
> Of too familiar happiness.

Wordsworth is too mature to point his finger at Shelley specifically and accuse him of immaturity. So, he cheerfully, and with characteristic, unflappable empathy, says 'we'. This is clever. Superficially, 'we' suggests that the poet considers himself to be on the same level as the Shelleys of the literary-political world. But, in coupling his former 'radical' self (the self he has apparently long since sloughed off) with the Shelleyan type as he is now, Wordsworth is quietly insisting, on a more important level, that *he* is the more dynamic and significant poet for having learned from his youthful experiences. His recollection of his, at bottom, inferior self (in comparison with his present self) having been seduced by the revolutionary fervour in 1790s France, detracts from any poet (like Shelley) who still harbours revolutionary ideas in 1820.

Shelley's disappointment with Wordsworth, at the latter's having become part of the conservative establishment from 1814 onwards, is usually the more fashionable of these two poets' ideological sentiments to indulge. But remember what Shelley (died 1822) did not get to know about Wordsworth: he never had the opportunity to read *The Borderers* (Wordsworth did not publish it until 1842); or the *Letter to the Bishop of Llandaff* (Wordsworth never published this at all); or *The Prelude* (this had been planned, by Wordsworth, to have been his posthumously played *ace*, so to speak). Yet even if one forgets about *The Borderers*, the *Letter to the Bishop of Llandaff* and *The Prelude*, Wordsworth's supposedly politically acquiescent, later poetry possesses unsung merit, if one knows where to look for it:

If this great world of joy and pain
Revolve in one sure track;
If freedom, set, will rise again,
And virtue, flown, come back;
Woe to the purblind crew who fill
The heart with each day's care;
Nor gain, from past or future, skill
To bear, and to forbear!

Composed in 1833, these lines show their author to be a poet who has gained a wise awareness of human nature, not in step with the urgent, fluctuating pulse-rate of political journalism, but against the backdrop of the changing seasons, the positions of heavenly bodies and the dark depth of the human heart. The sixty-three-year old poet still has the temerity to consider himself one of the real visionary noblesse. It is now impossible for the older Wordsworth, who has long been through his revolutionary phase, to be nudged into any particular rivulet of thought by ideologically motivated reportage. For a superior poet's mind to 'fill / The heart with each day's care'[8] is for it to stray too far amid the daily intricacies and petty details that should not concern it. For Wordsworth, to be out of touch with this truth (to be one of the 'purblind crew') is to be the plaything of political hacks whose irresponsible effusions circulate daily.

Some of Wordsworth's later poetry conceptualises the contemporary literary landscape as *his* terrain. He certainly feels himself to be aloof from the minuscule capacities for understanding possessed by readers unable to distinguish soaring genius from clod-like incapability:

> ... thou dost discern...
> No bold *bird* gone forth to forage
> 'Mid the tempest stern;
> But such mockery as the nations
> See, when public perturbations
> Lift men from their native stations,
> Like yon *tuft of fern*...

Remember that Wordsworth, in his capacity as a public poet, responds to criticism and the contemporary literary scene. Sometimes, far from being the literary advocate of mildewed Anglicanism, his later poetic voice bespeaks an attractive robustness and independence in his character. He has developed an immunity from the ideological feverishness that distorts the perceptions of those afflicted. His most important work – *The Prelude* – is under wraps It is his creation, which he handles with special, private care, doing his best to tailor it for literary immortality. The momentous nature of his poetic secret energises him for the cruder duties he feels are expected to be performed by the public Wordsworth. He may even sometimes caricature himself (or rather, his public self) in order to entertain readers. By now (1820), he is the man who has delighted some, and irritated others, since before the beginning of the century. In 'Hint From The Mountains', there is a metrically emphasised triteness about the lines that may signal Wordsworthian mischief. That is, he satirically valorizes the uncritical (urban) adulation of the daily bungling of commonplace writers who profess themselves contributors to human knowledge/wisdom. This is raillery of the most inspired variety that has not yet received its due. The man who gave you the *Lyrical Ballads*, fresh and authentic, from the land of lakes, mountains, and neglected and downtrodden – yet deep-thinking –

people will now (in 1820) offer you an equally valuable nugget of wisdom in four short and neat stanzas of gnomic precision. This poem says that, in terms of literary talent and how to judge it, not all that glitters is gold. A mediocre poet may utter a few inanities which, luckily for him, happen to flutter seductively on whichever unaccountable political breeze is causing 'public perturbations'.

This sort of promiscuous admiration, this approbation of the mob showered on far less deserving poets, would have been one of the most painful thorns in the younger Wordsworth's flesh. But now, having served his self-imposed writer's apprenticeship, he is cheerfully capable of countenancing the buzz created by the overrated literature of the moment. 'Hint From The Mountains' is as wry a look at the literary furore as any Thomas Love Peacock had published (two years earlier with *Nightmare Abbey*, or four years earlier with *Headlong Hall*). The kind of ecstasy voiced by universal admiration of mediocrity is placed between speech marks for the first half of this poem. This is Wordsworth's satirical glimpse of the foibles of the nation's readership:

> 'Mark him, how his power he uses,
> Lays it by, at will resumes!
> Mark, ere for his haunt he chooses
> Clouds and utter glooms!
> There he wheels in downward mazes;
> Sunward now his flight he raises,
> Catches fire, as seems, and blazes
> With uninjured plumes!'

The imaginary speaker, representative of (for Wordsworth) the typical reader of the time, is aroused by style while almost totally uninterested in content. Wordsworth knows that, as long as it struts its beautifully patterned plumage, intellectual aimlessness will be greeted by dullards' delight. In terms of how its imagery is conveyed, this (deliberately) has the cartoon quality of a Byron poem, or certain Shelley poems. Rather than labour his own irritability at his peers' condemnation of his later poetry, Wordsworth's poetic voice has become relaxed. He is now capable of a sort of droll equanimity that could only have been occasioned by those natural opiates released into the brain of a happy, healthy man who exercises regularly out of doors, and believes in himself. This is very different from the younger, more precious Wordsworth who had portrayed himself as more inclined to incubate his sensitivity.

The younger Wordsworth would not have dreamed of sullying his solidarity with all things rustic by composing the famous lines 'Upon Westminster Bridge' (1802), had it not been very early morning, when London is least characteristic of itself. In this poem, there is the sense that, because the city is now a *sleeping* beast, the poet may tentatively allow his sensitivity to brush ever so lightly against its teeth, talons and horns without being bitten, scraped or gored by any insidious spiritual depravity. Since he has shrugged the artifices of politics, society and other symptoms of human mismanagement off his back, he can only tolerate the benighted city when it is clothed in 'The beauty of the morning' and is 'silent, bare'. It is as if some mythical Hydra has been seen for the first time in a surprisingly unhorrifying light – a compromising position, even. The reader is invited to admire the component parts of an otherwise hideous creature, here observed between daily sixteen-hour bouts of frenetic materialism:

> Ships, towers, domes, theatres and temples lie
> Open unto the fields, and to the sky;
> All bright and glittering in the smokeless air.

The Wordsworthian sensitivity exclaims one last thing before scampering back out of reach of the coming day's sweaty, urban haste: 'Dear God! The very houses seem asleep; / And all that mighty heart is lying still!' Soon, the usual traffic will begin to rumble through narrow and insufficient streets. One will be flattened against walls by carriages from which the escutcheons and achievements of their owners will glow in coarse, heraldic tints...

It is just as well, for his own sanity's sake, that the later Wordsworth *did* become more relaxed in his approach to composition. He would hardly have outlived, as he did by decades, the whole Romantic movement for which he had been largely responsible, had he continued to wince at each and every vulgar, worldly reality.

Indeed, in 1820, he went on another tour of the continent, this time with his sister. Curiously, just as he had been disappointed, as a twenty-year-old, with seeing the Grande Chartreuse, Mont Blanc and Lake Geneva, so he would be disappointed, as a fifty-year-old, by many continental sights, such as that of the historical town, Aix-La- Chapelle:

> Why does this puny church present to view
> Her feeble columns? and that scanty chair!

This sword that one of our weak times might wear!
Objects of false pretence, or meanly true!

He is underwhelmed by the imaginative poverty embodied by the objects
present in a town of such major historical significance. The poet finds it
difficult to countenance the impoverished architecture, and even the
furniture. He does something important. The 'puny', 'feeble' and 'scanty'
nature of the scenery will hardly inspire high thinking. So he draws
extensively on his own mental resources in order to compensate for the
low quality of what is physically there. The fact that there is no actual
object there fit for his poetic contemplation is tantamount to his being let
down by his objective environment – again. Dorothy's account of their
arrival at Aix-La-Chapelle leaves us in no doubt as to how poor a sight the
place must have been:

> What an entrance to a city, the abode of Emperors, famed for
> its congresses of Princes, its Treaties, and its pomp of Priests
> and Churches, its baths, and its pleasures! Poverty stares upon
> you through big and wretched houses four or five stories high.
> From the wide shattered windows squalid half-naked women
> looked out after the rattling of our carriages.

Wordsworth must do all the work, as it were, to commune with the spirit in
European history, just as he alone had had to shoulder the unsettling burden
of the 'infinitude within' from 1790 until he met Coleridge, in 1797. By
1820, he has cultivated the mental poise to be able to deal with the glaring,
and potentially fatal, disproportion between his senses of outward vacancy
and his inner tumult. His own thoughts, about the history of the spot on
which he stands, are infinitely superior, as a source of spiritual edification,
to what he sees. He spurns the external scene, and in the most literal sense
of the phrase, enjoys *himself*:

> If from a traveller's fortune I might claim
> A palpable memorial of that day,
> Then would I seek the Pyrenean Breach
> That ROLAND clove with huge two-handed sway,
> And to the enormous labour left his name,
> Where unremitting frosts the rocky crescent bleach.

He thinks of the French hero whose real and legendary deeds of valour and chivalry inspired many medieval and later romances, including the eleventh century **Chanson de Roland** and Ariosto's **Orlando Furioso**. A knight of Charlemagne, indeed the greatest of the twelve legendary peers, Roland died most heroically, heading the rearguard during the retreat from Spain. For Wordsworth, his knowledge of the mighty events of the age of Charlemagne impoverish further, in his imagination, the squalid actuality of contemporary Aix-La-Chapelle. The sight of the cathedral city, where Charlemagne was born and buried, fails to satisfy Wordsworth's imaginative voracity, just as his imagination had been unsatisfied by the sight of the celebrated Alpine scenery thirty years before.

The fourteenth century town hall, containing the hall of the emperors, is built on the sight of Charlemagne's palace. Wordsworth's reaction to the 'Objects of false pretence, or meanly true!' is even one of indignation:

> Was it to disenchant and to undo
> That we approached the Seat of Charlemagne?
> To sweep from many an old romantic strain
> That faith which no devotion may renew!

Thirty years before, Wordsworth had been numbed, mentally, on his 1790 Alpine crossing, both by the sudden realisation of the sheer psychological abyss right inside him, and by the failure of spectacular external scenes to *help* him in some psychological (or spiritual) way. Now, in 1820, although he is the jaded sophisticate, he has once again been thrown back almost entirely onto his own resources, only this time to combat the isolation and lifelessness produced by the less daunting tyranny of more commonplace scenery.

On his 1790 walking tour, Wordsworth had felt the failure of Thomas Gray's celebrated reports of the spirituality which supposedly made its presence obvious at, say, the Grande Chartreuse. On his 1820 tour, Wordsworth feels failure in almost every man-made thing in view that *tries*, or *contrives*, to embody spirituality. Thirty years on, Wordsworth's poetry is still the poetry of disappointment. But, by now, that disappointment has settled in and around each and every wheel and cog of the compositional process, making his later output consist, mostly, of damp squibs. However, it is worth examining a couple more of these, because they indicate something significant about the poet. Look at 'In the Cathedral at Cologne':

O FOR the help of Angels to complete
This Temple – Angels governed by a plan
Thus far pursued (how gloriously!) by Man,
Studious that *He* might not disdain the seat
Who dwells in heaven! But that aspiring heat
Hath failed; and now, ye Powers! whose gorgeous wings
And splendid aspect yon emblazonings
But faintly picture, 'twere an office meet
For you, on these unfinished shafts to try
The midnight virtues of your harmony: –
This vast design might tempt you to repeat
Strains that call forth upon empyreal ground
Immortal Fabrics, rising to the sound
Of penetrating harps and voices sweet!

Wordsworth records how 'yon emblazonings/ But *faintly* picture' the gorgeous wings/ And splendid aspect' of heavenly angels. The poet feels that all these direct attempts, by men, at articulating otherworldly majesty, whether carved, painted, or written representations of actual spiritual beings, are the manifestations of a futile business. This is perhaps, also, an intellectual justification for the continued poetic activity of a largely uninspiring, middle-aged poet. But Wordsworth knows that the kind of artistic genius *really* capable of evoking spirituality rarely gives the viewer, or reader, more than a ray or two of otherworldly light at a time. It is almost a rule of thumb for Wordsworth that the works of mediocre poets, artists and architects will invariably protest too much on the side of spirituality. This is what makes his response, when he *is* eventually presented, on this 1820 tour, with the sight of a genuine masterpiece, so touchingly ecstatic.

Leonardo da Vinci's **Last Supper**, in the Refectory of the Convent of Santa Maria della Grazia in Milan, primes a more powerful detonation of holiness in the mind of the beholder than perfectly painted haloes or wings. For Wordsworth, **Last Supper** is a 'labour worthy of eternal youth!' because its power appears to have transcended, in some unique way, the silent assaults of decay and deliquescence, and their blind indifference towards Leonardo's endeavour, unseen, among the refectory wall's quarks and bosons, since it was painted upon it in about 1495. It still breathes a strange magic, an incantatory charm, which stirs Wordsworth to the depths of his being. Yet Leonardo's concentration on the *human* faces in Christ's company accords with Wordsworth's above-mentioned rule of thumb. **The**

Last Supper has somehow maintained its moral capacity to

> ... melt and thaw
> The heart of the Beholder – and erase
> (At least for one rapt moment) every trace
> Of disobedience to the primal law.

Despite centuries of her ruinous processes, nature has so far been unable to choke the triumph out of the artistry. The picture still has that force about it with which the very greatest art manages to reach the primitive seeds of humanity possessed alike by centuries of onlookers.

Wordsworth still longed to be able to send *his* art, beauty intact, far into the future, to connect with hearts and minds. His 1821 *Dedication*, accompanying his **Memorials of a Tour on the Continent**, illustrates this:

> ... Time halts not in his noiseless march –
> Nor turns, nor winds, as doth the liquid flood;
> Life slips from underneath us, like that arch
> Of airy workmanship whereon we stood,
> Earth stretched below, heaven in our neighbourhood.
> Go forth, my little Book! Pursue thy way;
> Go forth, and please the gentle and the good;
> Nor be a whisper stifled, if it say
> That treasures, yet untouched, may grace some future Lay.

About one century later, Ezra Pound, who would spearhead the Modernist movement alongside T. S. Eliot, would borrow this idea and dress it up – or rather, denude it – for more decadent poetic duties:

> Go, little naked and impudent songs,
> Go with a light foot!
> (Or with two light feet, if it please you!)
> Go and dance shamelessly!
> Go with an impertinent frolic!
> Greet the grave and the stodgy,
> Salute them with your thumbs at your noses...
>
> Dance and make people blush,
> Dance the dance of the phallus...

Ruffle the skirts of prudes,
    speak of their knees and ankles.
But, above all, go to practical people –
Say that you do no work
    and that you will live forever.
('Salutation the Second', from *Lustra*.)

The stage-management of one's posthumous presence in literature, though done often by artists of the twentieth century, is a characteristically Wordsworthian activity.

The vestigial atmosphere of Europe's troubled history clings unforgettably around some of the 1820 *Memorials*. The prospect of the field of Waterloo is 'blank and cold'. The 'wind-swept corn that wide around us rolled/ In dreary billows' is as dismal a wash of yellow as was ever conjured by a master of landscape painting. Amidst this spiritual desolation, the statues, in their mundane capacities as objects, somehow depreciate before the poet's eyes: '...monuments soon must disappear.' In other words, all human effort – including, of course, destructive effort – is inexorably subsumed by the pitilessly indifferent operations of the cosmos. Therefore, for Wordsworth, any sensitive English person should, by his contemplation of the monuments in the field at Waterloo, be humbled into a spiritually stimulating revaluation of human priorities. In this ideal event, he would naturally disincline himself, in future, from militaristic sentiments. 'If only', Wordsworth practically inwardly groans (all too aware that his fifty years of life have taught him the absolute certainty of quite the opposite), 'all the scoundrels, fools and warmongers could somehow be made to feel as *I* felt in the field at Waterloo':

Yet a dread local recompense we found;
While glory seemed betrayed, while patriot zeal
Sank in our hearts, we felt as men *should* feel.

Patriotic zeal *should* be made to sink in men's hearts. For Wordsworth, an ideal world would grow out of the hearts and minds of a human race whose each and every citizen could feel his 'patriot zeal' disarmed thus. After all, that moment in the field immerses those present in a natural and unprompted flood of truth. The British and Prussian forces, under the Duke of Wellington and Blücher, routed the French (under Napoleon) here, five years before, in 1815. But to vent any zealous patriotism in celebration of this military fact, on this spot, would be unimaginably churlish, 'With such vast hordes of hidden carnage near, / And horror breathing from the silent ground!' The somehow reproachful aspect of the former battleground is of the same poetic origins as the 'apt admonishment' that had been embodied in the fortuitous appearance of the leech-gatherer in *Resolution and Independence* (1802). If one were to focus one's patriotically motivated organs of sight on the battle monuments whilst remaining oblivious to the less objective, but infinitely more powerful, *feeling* that saturates the scene, one would be inhuman. Clearly, Wordsworth is still able to experience the admonitory power which comes from some natural, but opaque, source and moulds the receptive psyche. In the field at Waterloo, Wordsworth is *still* capable of being the childlike recipient of the kind of wisdom that cannot simply be intellectualised; nor can it be politicised: it is more important to be human than it is to be British, English, French, republican or conservative. Despite having boasted, in 1802, of the 'ancient English dower/ Of inward happiness', amongst his many other jingoistic gushings, the older Wordsworth is biased towards the same realm that had claimed his political allegiance in his 1798 *Lyrical Ballads* – humankind. It is just that, having accumulated, during the last two decades, a brain full of lamentably prosaic, but nevertheless painful and wearying experiences, he is not as light on his writing feet as the fighting-fit, slip of a poet he was. The inclination to rhapsodise readers out of their educated familiarity with the world has diminished. We are left with a poet condemned to a life of resignation and hard work, rather than some complacent writer.

Look at the 1818 piece, *Composed Upon an Evening of Extraordinary Splendour and Beauty*. In it, there is something poignant about the later Wordsworth's use of the very angels he had disdained to include in his more powerful spiritual effusions, such as his ode, *Intimations of Immortality From Recollections of Early Childhood*:

Time was when field and watery cove
With modulated echoes rang,
While choirs of fervent Angels sang
Their vespers in the grove...

And there is something worse than poignant about such exclamations as

Thine is the tranquil hour, purporeal Eve!

But there is much merit in this piece. A sunny haze is responsible for the seeming multiplication of mountain-ridges described in stanza three:

> And if there be whom broken ties
> Afflict, or injuries assail,
> Yon hazy ridges to their eyes
> Present a glorious scale,
> Climbing suffused with sunny air,
> To stop – no record has told where!

The natural phenomenon is likened, with laudable ingenuity, to Jacob's Ladder, leading to Heaven. In terms of poetic talent, Wordsworth still 'has it'. But 'it' – his ability to produce sublime analogies – has now become inextricably linked to his frequent inability to analogise an unfolding thought without ridiculousness creeping in. That is, the reader may well have enjoyed the Jacob's Ladder concept with the serious pleasure befitting the study of serious poetry, but how is he to feel about it all when he is, in the next breath, invited to picture the narrator suddenly sprout *wings*?

> And tempting Fancy to ascend,
> And with immortal Spirits blend!
> – Wings at my shoulders seem to play;
> But, rooted here, I stand and gaze
> On those bright steps that heavenward raise
> Their practicable way.

Presumably, a host of obvious poetic difficulties would have followed in the wake of the narrator *really* having to meet the rigours of effortless, newly angelic flapping. This is why those wings only '*seemed*' to play at his shoulders, for a non-committal moment. It is as if Wordsworth has remembered, just in the nick of time – or so he thinks he has – to conceal the silliness of a significant portion of his middle-aged thinking. He is like an austere schoolmaster who has, on wrongly supposing himself to be alone, and unwatched, during playtime, inadvertently allowed some of his young pupils to glimpse him sucking his thumb for comfort.

This demonstrates, all the more clearly, just how brilliant the poet, say, of the **Intimations** ode of 1802 must have been. In accordance with what could be argued to have been his self-fulfilling prophecy, the older Wordsworth has become a fully-grown man unable to 'see' the 'celestial light' in which his visions were once so majestically clothed:

There was a time when meadow, grove,
    and stream,
The earth, and every common sight,
    To me did seem
    Apparelled in celestial light,
The glory and the freshness of a dream.
It is not now as it hath been of yore; –
    Turn wheresoe'er I may,
    By night or day,
The things which I have seen I now can
    see no more.

    The Rainbow comes and goes,
    And lovely is the Rose,
    The Moon doth with delight
Look round her when the heavens are
    bare,
    Waters on a starry night
    Are beautiful and fair;
The sunshine is a glorious birth;
But yet I know, where'er I go,
That there hath past away a glory from
    the earth.

How strange it is that, when he wrote this, he was at his poetic best, yet it
rightly describes his future self's poetic perception as having faded 'into
the light of common day'.

However, there is little to be gained from smirking iconoclastically at
the useless sparks that flew around the older Wordsworth's well-used anvil.
Rather, one ought to celebrate such poems as his 'Extempore Effusion
Upon The Death Of James Hogg' (1835), which paid tribute to recently
deceased partners in the business of heavyweight thinking:

Nor has the rolling year twice measured,
From sign to sign, its steadfast course,
Since every mortal power of Coleridge
Was frozen at its marvellous source;

The rapt One, of the godlike forehead,
The heaven-eyed creature sleeps in earth:
And Lamb, the frolic and the gentle,
Has vanished from this lonely hearth.

This is as powerful as one of the *Silex Scintillans* (1660-65), with which
Henry Vaughan imagined his Hermetic philosopher brother, and other dead
beloved, to have 'gone into the world of light':

> I see them walking in an Air of glory,
>   Whose light doth trample on my days:
> My days, which are at best but dull and hoary,
>   Meer glimering and decays.

But the occasional *scintillas* of the older Wordsworth, struck as they are
amidst the increasingly train-timetabled, smoke-filled, climate of a rapidly
industrialising England, effect the fantail of adapted sensibility:

> Like clouds that rake the mountain-summits,
> Or waves that own no curbing hand,
> How fast has brother followed brother,
> From sunshine to the sunless land!
>
> Yet I, whose lids from infant slumber
> Were earlier raised, remain to hear
> A timid voice, that asks in whispers,
> "Who next will drop and disappear?"
>
> Our haughty life is crowned with darkness,
> Like London with its own black wreath,
> On which with thee, O Crabbe! forth-looking,
> I gazed from Hampstead's breezy heath.

X – In Conclusion

Better a faded Wordsworth than never a burst of light. The blaze of each of his critical immolations, at the hands of more generations than not since he proclaimed his presence in 1798, throws unmistakable light on an incomparable icon.

Yes, he did very often write badly as an older man (and as a younger man). Yes, he did allow moral considerations to interfere with aesthetic perceptions. But he *did* lie, cheat, deceive, and be untrue to nature and contemptuous of history. In other words, he was himself – and a true artist. This short study has been an attempt to present him, with all his unscrupulous brilliance, and all his impudent theocentrism, with the contradictions intact. As Michael Baron says in his *Language and Relationship in Wordsworth's Writing* (Longman, 1995): 'How can a poet be so revered *and* so largely neglected? It is hard to think of a comparable case.'

James Stephens's poem presents to posterity a deliciously absurd Jekyll and Hyde portrait of Wordsworth the artist: 'Two voices are there... One is of the deep... and one is of an old half-witted sheep, and Wordsworth, both are thine.' This is entertaining; as entertaining as Jeffrey's journalistic excellence at being Wordsworth's primary intellectual saboteur. But it is to the genius Coleridge that the last word should be given, not least because Coleridge willingly absorbed himself into Wordsworth's thinking, in order that this most criticised great would eventually receive his laurel:

> Parodies on new poems are read as satires; on old ones – the
> soliloquy of Hamlet for instance – as compliments. A man of
> genius may securely laugh at a mode of attack by which his
> reviler, in half a century or less, becomes his encomiast.

Wordsworth banged Cowper's and Blake's heads together, and from the descriptive éclat of one and the dogmatic liberalism of the other, made poetry a philosophy that could look the next two centuries in the eye.

Footnotes

1 Samuel Taylor Coleridge.
2 'The Contemporaneity of the *Lyrical Ballads*' (1954).
3 From Danby's 1960 essay, '*Simon Lee*' and '*The Idiot Boy.*'
4 From Christiansen's entertaining survey of the Romantic era, *Romantic Affinities.*
5 Moorman's *William Wordsworth: The Later Years.*
6 In 'Vision' in *Door into the Dark.*
7 In Fowler's *A History of English Literature* (Blackwell, 1989).
8 From 'If this great world of joy and pain…' (1833).

Select Bibliography

Editions:
William Wordsworth (The *Oxford Authors Series*), edited by Stephen Gill, 1984.

The Prelude (The 1805 Text), edited from the manuscripts with an Introduction and notes by Ernest DeSelincourt. Corrected by Stephen Gill, Oxford, 1970.

(De Selincourt's short study of the 'evolution' of *The Prelude*, from 1805 to 1850, is very revealing.)

Wordsworth: Selected Poems, edited with an Introduction and notes by H.M. Margoliouth, Collins, 1992.

(Includes the great Preface to *Lyrical Ballads*, and the Intro. is an absorbing, 'potted', biographical/critical study of Wordsworth.)

The Works of William Wordsworth, Wordsworth Poetry Library, 1994.

The Prose Works of William Wordsworth (3 vols), edited by Rev. Alexander B. Grosart, Moxon, 1876.

(Includes so much – earlier Wordsworthian polemics, and pen-portraits of the poet by lively writers of the time – that it is simply irreplaceable.)

(Coleridge) Editions:
Poems and Prose Selected By Kathleen Raine, Penguin, 1957.

(Includes the best of the *Biographia Literaria*.)

The Works of Samuel Taylor Coleridge, Wordsworth Poetry Library, 1994.

Biographical/Critical:
John Beer, *Wordsworth In Time*, Faber, 1979.

A.S. Byatt, *Wordsworth and Coleridge in Their Time*, Nelson, 1970.

Stephen Gill, *William Wordsworth: A Life*, Oxford, 1989.

Kenneth R. Johnston, *The Hidden Wordsworth: Poet Lover Rebel Spy*, Norton, 1998.

(Not so much for its controversial nature as its sheer wealth of compelling detail.)

Mary Moorman, *William Wordsworth: A Biography* (2 vols), Oxford, 1957, 1965.

Ernest De Selincourt, *Dorothy Wordsworth*, Oxford, 1933.

More General:
Marilyn Butler, *Romantics, Rebels & Reactionaries*, Oxford, 1981.
(Highly perceptive cultural analysis of the so-called 'Romantic' era, utterly undeceived by the myths and mists created by the writers. A real political eye-opener.)
Rupert Christiansen, *Romantic Affinities*, Vintage, 1994.

GREENWICH EXCHANGE BOOKS

LITERARY SERIES

The Greenwich Exchange Literary Series is a collection of critical essays of major or contemporary serious writers in English and selected European languages. The series is for the student, the teacher and 'common readers' and is an ideal resource for libraries. The *Times Educational Supplement* praised these books, saying, "The style of [this series] has a pressure of meaning behind it. Readers should learn from that ... If art is about selection, perception and taste, then this is it."

(ISBN prefix 1-871551- applies)
All books are paperbacks unless otherwise stated

The series includes:
W.H. Auden by Stephen Wade (36-6)
Honoré de Balzac by Wendy Mercer (48-X)
William Blake by Peter Davies (27-7)
The Brontës by Peter Davies (24-2)
Robert Browning by John Lucas (59-5)
Byron by Andrew Keanie (83-9)
Samuel Taylor Coleridge by Andrew Keanie (64-1)
Joseph Conrad by Martin Seymour-Smith (18-8)
William Cowper by Michael Thorn (25-0)
Charles Dickens by Robert Giddings (26-9)
Emily Dickinson by Marnie Pomeroy (68-4)
John Donne by Sean Haldane (23-4)
Ford Madox Ford by Anthony Fowles (63-3)
The Stagecraft of Brian Friel by David Grant (74-9)
Robert Frost by Warren Hope (70-6)
Thomas Hardy by Sean Haldane (33-1)
Seamus Heaney by Warren Hope (37-4)
Joseph Heller by Anthony Fowles (84-6)
Gerard Manley Hopkins by Sean Sheehan (77-3)
James Joyce by Michael Murphy (73-0)
Laughter in the Dark – The Plays of Joe Orton by Arthur Burke (56-0)
Philip Larkin by Warren Hope (35-8)
Poets of the First World War by John Greening (79-X)
Philip Roth by Paul McDonald (72-2)
Shakespeare's *Macbeth* by Matt Simpson (69-2)

Shakespeare's *Othello* by Matt Simpson (71-4)
Shakespeare's *The Tempest* by Matt Simpson (75-7)
Shakespeare's *Twelfth Night* by Matt Simpson (86-2)
Shakespeare's Non-Dramatic Poetry by Martin Seymour-Smith (22-6)
Shakespeare's Sonnets by Martin Seymour-Smith (38-2)
Shakespeare's *The Winter's Tale* by John Lucas (80-3)
Tobias Smollett by Robert Giddings (21-8)
Dylan Thomas by Peter Davies (78-1)
Alfred, Lord Tennyson by Michael Thorn (20-X)
William Wordsworth by Andrew Keanie (57-9)
W.B. Yeats by John Greening (34-X)

LITERATURE & BIOGRAPHY

Matthew Arnold and 'Thyrsis' *by Patrick Carill Connolly*
Matthew Arnold (1822-1888) was a leading poet, intellect and aesthete of the Victorian epoch. He is now best known for his strictures as a literary and cultural critic, and educationist. After a long period of neglect, his views have come in for a re-evaluation. Arnold's poetry remains less well known, yet his poems and his understanding of poetry, which defied the conventions of his time, were central to his achievement.

The author traces Arnold's intellectual and poetic development, showing how his poetry gathers its meanings from a lifetime's study of European literature and philosophy. Connolly's unique exegesis of 'Thyrsis' draws upon a wide-ranging analysis of the pastoral and its associated myths in both classical and native cultures. This study shows lucidly and in detail how Arnold encouraged the intense reflection of the mind on the subject placed before it, believing in " ... the all importance of the choice of the subject, the necessity of accurate observation; and subordinate character of expression."

Patrick Carill Connolly gained his English degree at Reading University and taught English literature abroad for a number of years before returning to Britain. He is now a civil servant living in London.
2004 • 180 pages • ISBN 1-871551-61-7

The Author, the Book and the Reader *by Robert Giddings*
This collection of essays analyses the effects of changing technology and the attendant commercial pressures on literary styles and subject matter. Authors covered include Charles Dickens, Tobias Smollett, Mark Twain, Dr Johnson and John le Carré.
1991 • 220 pages • illustrated • ISBN 1-871551-01-3

Aleister Crowley and the Cult of Pan *by Paul Newman*
Few more nightmarish figures stalk English literature than Aleister Crowley (1875-1947), poet, magician, mountaineer and agent provocateur. In this groundbreaking study, Paul Newman dives into the occult mire of Crowley's works and fishes out gems and grotesqueries that are by turns ethereal, sublime, pornographic and horrifying. Like Oscar Wilde before him, Crowley stood in "symbolic relationship to his age" and to contemporaries like Rupert Brooke, G.K. Chesterton and the Portuguese modernist, Fernando Pessoa. An influential exponent of the cult of the Great God Pan, his essentially 'pagan' outlook was shared by major European writers as well as English novelists like E.M. Forster, D.H. Lawrence and Arthur Machen.
Paul Newman lives in Cornwall. Editor of the literary magazine *Abraxas*, he has written over ten books.
2004 • 222 pages • ISBN 1-871551-66-8

John Dryden *by Anthony Fowles*
Of all the poets of the Augustan age, John Dryden was the most worldly. Anthony Fowles traces Dryden's evolution from 'wordsmith' to major poet.
This critical study shows a poet of vigour and technical panache whose art was forged in the heat and battle of a turbulent polemical and pamphleteering age. Although Dryden's status as a literary critic has long been established, Fowles draws attention to his neglected achievements as a translator of poetry. He deals also with the less well-known aspects of Dryden's work – his plays and occasional pieces.
Born in London and educated at the Universities of Oxford and Southern California, Anthony Fowles began his career in film-making before becoming an author of film and television scripts and more than twenty books. Readers will welcome the many contemporary references to novels and film with which Fowles illuminates the life and work of this decisively influential English poetic voice.
2003 • 292 pages • ISBN 1-871551-58-7

The Good That We Do *by John Lucas*
John Lucas' book blends fiction, biography and social history in order to tell the story of his grandfather, Horace Kelly. Headteacher of a succession of elementary schools in impoverished areas of London, 'Hod' Kelly was also a keen cricketer, a devotee of the music hall, and included among his friends the great trade union leader Ernest Bevin. In telling the story of his life, Lucas has provided a fascinating range of insights into the lives of ordinary Londoners from the First World War until the outbreak of the Second World War. Threaded throughout is an account of such people's hunger for education, and of the different ways government, church and educational officialdom

ministered to that hunger. *The Good That We Do* is both a study of one man and of a period when England changed, drastically and forever.

John Lucas is Professor Emeritus of the Universities of Loughborough and Nottingham Trent. He is the author of numerous works of a critical and scholarly nature and has published seven collections of poetry.

2001 • 214 pages • ISBN 1-871551-54-4

In Pursuit of Lewis Carroll *by Raphael Shaberman*
Sherlock Holmes and the author uncover new evidence in their investigations into the mysterious life and writing of Lewis Carroll. They examine published works by Carroll that have been overlooked by previous commentators. A newly-discovered poem, almost certainly by Carroll, is published here.

Amongst many aspects of Carroll's highly complex personality, this book explores his relationship with his parents, numerous child friends, and the formidable Mrs Liddell, mother of the immortal Alice. Raphael Shaberman was a founder member of the Lewis Carroll Society and a teacher of autistic children.

1994 • 118 pages • illustrated • ISBN 1-871551-13-7

Liar! Liar!: Jack Kerouac – Novelist *by R.J. Ellis*
The fullest study of Jack Kerouac's fiction to date. It is the first book to devote an individual chapter to every one of his novels. *On the Road*, *Visions of Cody* and *The Subterraneans* are reread in-depth, in a new and exciting way. *Visions of Gerard* and *Doctor Sax* are also strikingly reinterpreted, as are other daringly innovative writings, like 'The Railroad Earth' and his "try at a spontaneous *Finnegans Wake*" – *Old Angel Midnight*. Neglected writings, such as *Tristessa* and *Big Sur*, are also analysed, alongside better-known novels such as *Dharma Bums* and *Desolation Angels*.

R.J. Ellis is Senior Lecturer in English at Nottingham Trent University.

1999 • 294 pages • ISBN 1-871551-53-6

Musical Offering *by Yolanthe Leigh*
In a series of vivid sketches, anecdotes and reflections, Yolanthe Leigh tells the story of her growing up in the Poland of the 1930s and the Second World War. These are poignant episodes of a child's first encounters with both the enchantments and the cruelties of the world; and from a later time, stark memories of the brutality of the Nazi invasion, and the hardships of student life in Warsaw under the Occupation. But most of all this is a record of inward development; passages of remarkable intensity and simplicity describe the girl's response to religion, to music, and to her discovery of philosophy.

Yolanthe Leigh was formerly a Lecturer in Philosophy at Reading University.

2000 • 56 pages • ISBN: 1-871551-46-3

Norman Cameron *by Warren Hope*
Norman Cameron's poetry was admired by W.H. Auden, celebrated by Dylan Thomas and valued by Robert Graves. He was described by Martin Seymour-Smith as, "one of ... the most rewarding and pure poets of his generation ..." and is at last given a full-length biography. This eminently sociable man, who had periods of darkness and despair, wrote little poetry by comparison with others of his time, but it is always of a consistently high quality – imaginative and profound.
2000 • 220 pages • illustrated • ISBN 1-871551-05-6

POETRY

Adam's Thoughts in Winter *by Warren Hope*
Warren Hope's poems have appeared from time to time in a number of literary periodicals, pamphlets and anthologies on both sides of the Atlantic. They appeal to lovers of poetry everywhere. His poems are brief, clear, frequently lyrical, characterised by wit, but often distinguished by tenderness. The poems gathered in this first book-length collection counter the brutalising ethos of contemporary life, speaking of, and for, the virtues of modesty, honesty and gentleness in an individual, memorable way.
2000 • 46 pages • ISBN 1-871551-40-4

Baudelaire: Les Fleurs du Mal *Translated by F.W. Leakey*
Selected poems from *Les Fleurs du Mal* are translated with parallel French texts and are designed to be read with pleasure by readers who have no French as well as those who are practised in the French language.
F.W. Leakey was Professor of French in the University of London. As a scholar, critic and teacher he specialised in the work of Baudelaire for 50 years and published a number of books on the poet.
2001 • 152 pages • ISBN 1-871551-10-2

'The Last Blackbird' and other poems by Ralph Hodgson *edited and introduced by John Harding*
Ralph Hodgson (1871-1962) was a poet and illustrator whose most influential and enduring work appeared to great acclaim just prior to, and during, the First World War. His work is imbued with a spiritual passion for the beauty of creation and the mystery of existence. This new selection brings together, for the first time in 40 years, some of the most beautiful and powerful 'hymns to life' in the English language.
John Harding lives in London. He is a freelance writer and teacher and is Ralph Hodgson's biographer.
2004 • 70 pages • ISBN 1-871551-81-1

Lines from the Stone Age *by Sean Haldane*
Reviewing Sean Haldane's 1992 volume *Desire in Belfast*, Robert Nye wrote in *The Times* that "Haldane can be sure of his place among the English poets." This place is not yet a conspicuous one, mainly because his early volumes appeared in Canada, and because he has earned his living by other means than literature. Despite this, his poems have always had their circle of readers. The 60 previously unpublished poems of *Lines from the Stone Age* – "lines of longing, terror, pride, lust and pain" – may widen this circle.
2000 • 52 pages • ISBN 1-871551-39-0

Shakespeare's Sonnets *by Martin Seymour-Smith*
Martin Seymour-Smith's outstanding achievement lies in the field of literary biography and criticism. In 1963 he produced his comprehensive edition, in the old spelling, of *Shakespeare's Sonnets* (here revised and corrected by himself and Peter Davies in 1998). With its landmark introduction and its brilliant critical commentary on each sonnet, it was praised by William Empson and John Dover Wilson. Stephen Spender said of him "I greatly admire Martin Seymour-Smith for the independence of his views and the great interest of his mind"; and both Robert Graves and Anthony Burgess described him as the leading critic of his time. His exegesis of the *Sonnets* remains unsurpassed.
2001 • 194 pages • ISBN 1-871551-38-2

The Rain and the Glass *by Robert Nye*
When Robert Nye's first poems were published, G.S. Fraser declared in the *Times Literary Supplement*: "Here is a proper poet, though it is hard to see how the larger literary public (greedy for flattery of their own concerns) could be brought to recognize that. But other proper poets – how many of them are left? – will recognize one of themselves."
Since then Nye has become known to a large public for his novels, especially *Falstaff* (1976), winner of the Hawthornden Prize and The Guardian Fiction Prize, and *The Late Mr Shakespeare* (1998). But his true vocation has always been poetry, and it is as a poet that he is best known to his fellow poets. "Nye is the inheritor of a poetic tradition that runs from Donne and Ralegh to Edward Thomas and Robert Graves," wrote James Aitchison in 1990, while the critic Gabriel Josipovici has described him as "one of the most interesting poets writing today, with a voice unlike that of any of his contemporaries".
This book contains all the poems Nye has written since his *Collected Poems* of 1995, together with his own selection from that volume. An introduction, telling the story of his poetic beginnings, affirms Nye's unfashionable belief in inspiration, as well as defining that quality of unforced truth which

distinguishes the best of his work: "I have spent my life trying to write poems, but the poems gathered here came mostly when I was not."
2005 • 132 pages • ISBN 1-871551-41-2

Wilderness *by Martin Seymour-Smith*
This is Martin Seymour-Smith's first publication of his poetry for more than twenty years. This collection of 36 poems is a fearless account of an inner life of love, frustration, guilt, laughter and the celebration of others. He is best known to the general public as the author of the controversial and bestselling *Hardy* (1994).
1994 • 52 pages • ISBN 1-871551-08-0

BUSINESS

English Language Skills *by Vera Hughes*
If you want to be sure, (as a student, or in your business or personal life), that your written English is correct, this book is for you. Vera Hughes' aim is to help you to remember the basic rules of spelling, grammar and punctuation. 'Noun', 'verb', 'subject', 'object' and 'adjective' are the only technical terms used. The book teaches the clear, accurate English required by the business and office world. It coaches acceptable current usage and makes the rules easier to remember.
Vera Hughes was a civil servant and is a trainer and author of training manuals.
2002 • 142 pages • ISBN 1-871551-60-9